Castro's Cuba

Castro's Cuba

Other books in the History Firsthand series:

Castro's Cuba

Charles W. Carey Jr., *Book Editor*

Bonnie Szumski, *Publisher*
Scott Barbour, *Managing Editor*
David M. Haugen, *Series Editor*

GREENHAVEN
PRESS®

THOMSON

GALE

San Diego • Detroit • New York • San Francisco • Cleveland
New Haven, Conn. • Waterville, Maine • London • Munich

© 2004 by Greenhaven Press. Greenhaven Press is an imprint of The Gale Group, Inc., a division of Thomson Learning, Inc.

Greenhaven® and Thomson Learning™ are trademarks used herein under license.

For more information, contact
Greenhaven Press
27500 Drake Rd.
Farmington Hills, MI 48331-3535
Or you can visit our Internet site at http://www.gale.com

Cover credit: © Richard Bickel/CORBIS
Corel Corporation, 165
Library of Congress, 17, 41

LIBRARY OF CONGRESS CATALOGING-IN-PUBLICATION DATA

Castro's Cuba / Charles W. Carey Jr., book editor.
   p. cm. — (History firsthand)
   Includes bibliographical references and index.
   ISBN 0-7377-1654-1 (lib. : alk. paper) — ISBN 0-7377-1655-X (pbk. : alk. paper)
      1. Cuba—Economic conditions—1959– . 2. Cuba—Economic policy.
   3. Cuba—Social conditions—1959– . 4. Socialism—Cuba. 5. Cuba—Politics
   and government—1959– . 6. Cuba—History—Revolution, 1959. I. Carey,
   Charles W., Jr. II. Series.
   HC152.5.C383 2004
   330.97291'064—dc22   2003047286

Printed in the United States of America

Contents

ate Cuban invaders at Playa Girón, or the Bay of Pigs, in 1961.

Chapter 3: Justice for All

Chapter 4: Surviving Without Soviet Aid

Foreword

In his preface to a book on the events leading to the Civil War, Stephen B. Oates, the historian and biographer of Abraham Lincoln, John Brown, and other noteworthy American historical figures, explained the difficulty of writing history in the traditional third-person voice of the biographer and historian. "The trouble, I realized, was the detached third-person voice," wrote Oates. "It seemed to wring all the life out of my characters and the antebellum era." Indeed, how can a historian, even one as prominent as Oates, compete with the eloquent voices of Daniel Webster, Abraham Lincoln, Harriet Beecher Stowe, Frederick Douglass, and Robert E. Lee?

Oates's comment notwithstanding, every student of history, professional and amateur alike, can name a score of excellent accounts written in the traditional third-person voice of the historian that bring to life an event or an era and the people who lived through it. In *Battle Cry of Freedom*, James M. McPherson vividly re-creates the American Civil War. Barbara Tuchman's *The Guns of August* captures in sharp detail the tensions in Europe that led to the outbreak of World War I. Taylor Branch's *Parting the Waters* provides a detailed and dramatic account of the American Civil Rights Movement. The study of history would be impossible without such guiding texts.

Nonetheless, Oates's comment makes a compelling point. Often the most convincing tellers of history are those who lived through the event, the eyewitnesses who recorded their firsthand experiences in autobiographies, speeches, memoirs, journals, and letters. The Greenhaven Press History Firsthand series presents history through the words of first-person narrators. Each text in this series captures a significant historical era or event—the American Civil War, the

Great Depression, the Holocaust, the Roaring Twenties, the 1960s, the Vietnam War. Readers will investigate these historical eras and events by examining primary-source documents, authored by chroniclers both famous and little known. The texts in the History Firsthand series comprise the celebrated and familiar words of the presidents, generals, and famous men and women of letters who recorded their impressions for posterity, as well as the statements of the ordinary people who struggled to understand the storm of events around them—the foot soldiers who fought the great battles and their loved ones back home, the men and women who waited on the breadlines, the college students who marched in protest.

The texts in this series are particularly suited to students beginning serious historical study. By examining these first-hand documents, novice historians can begin to form their own insights and conclusions about the historical era or event under investigation. To aid the student in that process, the texts in the History Firsthand series include introductions that provide an overview of the era or event, timelines, and bibliographies that point the serious student toward key historical works for further study.

The study of history commences with an examination of words—the testimony of witnesses who lived through an era or event and left for future generations the task of making sense of their accounts. The Greenhaven Press History Firsthand series invites the beginner historian to commence the process of historical investigation by focusing on the words of those individuals who made history by living through it and recording their experiences firsthand.

Introduction: Castro and Revolutionized Cuba

The Cuban Revolution of 1959 was a major turning point in the history of that island nation. Before the revolution, Cuba's economy revolved around the cultivation of sugar, tobacco, and tropical fruits, most of which were sold to the United States. The economy was dominated by a small group of Cuban landowners and foreign corporations, such as the United Fruit Company, which raked in huge profits from their operations. Meanwhile, millions of cane cutters and their families were forced to make do on the wages they earned during the four-month sugar harvest. Politically, the government was firmly in the hands of wealthy land-owning conservatives who did more to serve the interests of foreign investors—and themselves—than they did those of the Cuban people. Most Cuban workers lived in poverty while the elite sported with American tourists in Havana. As Louis A. Pérez Jr. put it,

> Daily life had developed into a relentless degradation, with the complicity of political leaders and public officials who operated at the behest of U.S. interests. The reputation of Cuba as the "red light district of the Caribbean," the "Las Vegas of Latin America," the "brothel of the New World," offended Cuban sensibilities.[1]

After the revolution most of the wealthy and professional classes emigrated, the holdings of the foreign corporations were nationalized, the casinos and brothels were shut down, and the island's wealth was redistributed to raise the standard of living for the masses. The Soviet Union took the place of the United States as the major customer for Cuban agricultural products. Politically, Cuba became a base camp from which the Socialist revolution could spread throughout the rest of Latin America, and those Cubans who disagreed with the revolution were oppressed, much the same way they were by the prerevolution regime.

Revolt of the Sergeants

The first of several events leading up to the Cuban revolution took place in 1933, when the government of Gerardo Machado was overthrown. The rebels were led by Fulgencio Batista, a sergeant in the Cuban army, but drew heavily on the ranks of students and professional men for support. Many of the reforms they demanded, and for a time implemented, were similar to those that the Revolution of 1959 would later establish.

The government that replaced Machado accomplished a great deal during its tenure. It nullified the Platt Amendment in the Cuban constitution, which gave the United States the right to interfere in Cuban internal affairs and to dictate its foreign affairs. It also gave women the right to vote, established an eight-hour workday and a department of labor, opened the universities to the poor, implemented a program of land reform, and nationalized the U.S.-owned electric companies. Many of these reforms were undone by succeeding governments, but initially they helped galvanize the Cuban people to press for greater control over their government and a greater share of the island's wealth.

The Constitution of 1940

The Revolt of the Sergeants, as the 1933 revolution was known, set in motion a process of liberalization that culminated in a new constitution. The constitution of 1940 guaranteed individual and social rights, supported full employment and a minimum wage, extended social security to many seasonal workers, and called for equal pay for equal work. It also provided for land reforms by outlawing the *latifundias*, the large plantations owned by a handful of Cubans and foreign corporations, and called on the government to curb the influence of foreign corporations over the Cuban economy.

The constitution failed to provide the means by which

these reforms could be accomplished, and so its promise remained largely unfulfilled. However, the 1940 constitution established goals toward which Cubans could strive as a way to improve the material circumstances of their lives. Its suspension in 1952 was the direct cause of the Cuban revolution.

The Batista Regime

One of the driving forces behind the adoption of the 1940 constitution was Fulgencio Batista. From 1933, when he engineered the Revolt of the Sergeants, until 1959, when he stepped down as prime minister, Batista was the leading figure in Cuban politics. At first he was a true reformer, and he expanded the educational system, implemented a major public works program, and fostered economic growth. By 1952, however, Batista had become more conservative. That same year he suspended the constitution and declared himself a dictator. For the next seven years he ruled Cuba with a heavy hand, in much the same way as had Machado.

Batista's actions drove a number of Cubans to work actively for his overthrow, among them a young lawyer named Fidel Castro. Castro had been a candidate for the Cuban parliament in the elections of 1952, which Batista had also suspended, and he set out to get rid of the dictator and restore the 1940 constitution.

Castro Starts a Revolution

On July 26, 1953, Castro and two hundred fellow revolutionaries attacked Moncada military barracks in Santiago de Cuba, where one thousand government troops were stationed. The assault was a miserable failure; most of the attackers were killed, and Castro and the surviving rebels were sentenced to ten-year prison terms. After serving two years of his term, Castro was exiled to Mexico. From Mexico City he began to plot another attempt at revolution.

In 1956 Castro returned, but he was not much better prepared than before. His band of eighty-two revolutionaries left Mexico in a pleasure yacht named *Granma* and landed on a swampy beach in Oriente Province just west of the city of

Santiago de Cuba. The Cuban military had been notified by Mexican authorities that the rebels were on their way, and most of Castro's people were rounded up or killed within a week. The dozen or so survivors took refuge in the Sierra Maestra mountain range and began recruiting disillusioned peasants to their cause, which became known as the July 26th Movement. Meanwhile, other revolutionary groups, including the Popular Socialist Party, began organizing students and urban workers to depose Batista. By 1959 more than one thousand guerrillas were actively fighting against the Batista regime, and they were supported by thousands more dissidents in the cities and countryside.

Castro Takes Command

Despite their small numbers the rebels were able to keep Cuba in a state of constant turmoil. This was because Batista's army was poorly equipped, trained, and led, and had little desire to fight for the dictator. Castro's rebels won several impressive victories over Batista's army, and they gradually took control of Oriente Province. Meanwhile, other rebel groups, such as the March 13th Revolutionary Directorate, began guerrilla operations in other parts of the island. Batista's inability to quash the revolt cost him the support of the Cuban elite, and on January 1, 1959, he relinquished his office and fled to the Dominican Republic.

As Jaime Suchlicki has noted, "Castro's charisma and his revolutionary prestige made him, in the eyes of the Cuban people, the logical occupant of Batista's chair; he was the man of the hour, the new messiah."[2] Castro formed the various rebel factions, including the Popular Socialist Party and the March 13th Revolutionary Directorate, into one political party and took control of Cuba as the prime minister. For the next forty years he oversaw the transition of Cuba's society and economy from neocolonialism to communism.

The first move in this direction was the May 1959 Agrarian Reform Law. The law outlawed foreign land ownership and prohibited any individual from owning more than 160 acres. Excess acreage was appropriated by the government and converted into *granjas*, or state farms. Landless peasants were assigned to the farms, given year-round rather than seasonal work, and paid a small salary and a share of the profits. Small landowners were allowed to continue farming on their own and sell their produce in free farmers' markets. As late as the 1990s almost 10 percent of the country's farmland was operated privately, although the free farmers' markets had been closed in 1986 because the prof-

Fidel Castro (seated) and two armed followers take refuge in the Sierra Maestra mountain range in eastern Cuba's Oriente Province.

its private farmers were earning created discontent among *granja* workers. However, all farmers, private and collective, were included in the nation's social welfare programs, so that the quality of their lives rose significantly.

In 1960 the Urban Reform Law outlawed the rental of private property, including apartments and houses. As a result many urban Cubans gained ownership of their living quarters, while others paid substantially reduced rents. That same year the government nationalized more than three hundred of the largest Cuban-owned firms. Workers were guaranteed year-round employment and had their wages increased, and they were included under the umbrella of state-funded social welfare programs.

The Revolution Implements Social Programs

The income from agrarian reform and nationalization provided the funds to finance major social welfare programs. Housing for the poor was upgraded via a massive project to construct low-income housing, particularly in rural areas, and to electrify much of the countryside. This allowed many peasants to leave their rickety shacks behind and move into modest but modern living accommodations. Education was improved by nationalizing the nation's many private and religious schools and opening their doors to all children at no charge. This initiative soon contributed to the elimination of illiteracy from the island, which had been about 30 percent before the revolution. As part of the literacy initiative the government established public libraries across the island. By 1989 the number of libraries had increased from approximately one hundred in 1959 to more than two thousand.

The government also set out to provide free medical treatment for all Cubans. The mass emigration of medical doctors made this initiative difficult to achieve at first, but eventually Cuban universities were turning out more than enough trained medical personnel to handle the demand. By 1989 every Cuban received whatever medical care was needed, regardless of the cost and without having to pay.

Anti-Castro Dissidents Emigrate

As a result of these measures, the standard of living of the rural and urban working class increased substantially. However, as Jesús Arboleya has noted, "lowering rents and electricity and telephone rates, increasing minimum salary, and other measures benefiting the working sectors openly clashed with the interests of the privileged few."[3] As the standard of living of the masses rose, the middle and upper classes lost much of their wealth, so much so that many well-to-do people began leaving Cuba. Virtually all of the upper class and much of the small middle class, including a majority of the nation's medical doctors, teachers, and engineers, fled the country with as much of their wealth as they could carry off.

Many émigrés settled in Latin America and Spain, but a good number relocated to south Florida. Once in the United States, they complained bitterly and loudly to the U.S. government to do something about Castro. They also formed associations, such as the Cuban-American National Foundation, to lobby Congress on behalf of Cuban expatriates. Some of these groups also planned and funded air raids, industrial sabotage, and other counterrevolutionary acts of terror in Cuba.

Emigration rid Cuba of its counterrevolutionaries and helped secure the revolution's success. Emigration also contributed to a worsening of relations between Cuba and the United States, by far its most important trading partner. Cuba's primary export was sugar, and the United States bought most of what the island produced. In the wake of the emigrations the U.S. government began to fear that the revolution was becoming increasingly socialistic, and it put pressure on Castro to liberalize and democratize his regime.

U.S.-Cuban Relations Deteriorate

Meanwhile, Castro had begun talking with the Soviet Union in an effort to expand the market for Cuban sugar, thus reducing Cuba's dependency on one big customer. In 1960 the Soviets eagerly agreed to take large quantities of sugar in exchange for Soviet crude oil. The deal was a good one for Castro, since Cuba produced only about 10 percent of its petroleum needs. But it set off a chain of events that eventually restricted Cuban trade tremendously, a restriction from which it never recovered.

Most of the island's oil refineries were owned by American petroleum companies. At the strong urging of the U.S. government, which feared having a Socialist regime so close to home, they refused to refine the Soviet crude oil when it arrived. The refusal left Castro with little choice but to nationalize the refineries. In retaliation, in 1960 the U.S. government declared a total trade embargo against Cuba, whereupon Castro nationalized the remaining holdings of American companies. These holdings included approximately 90 percent of Cuba's mines, 80 percent of its public utilities, 50 percent of its railways, 40 percent of its sugar production, and 25 percent of its bank deposits.

The emigrations and the embargo had a profound effect on Cuban society. For several years medical care declined because of the shortage of doctors, more than half of whom had emigrated after Castro's takeover. Medical care was further complicated by the fact that most prescription drug patents are held by U.S. pharmaceutical corporations, and these corporations were now prohibited by law from exporting modern medicines to Cuba. Likewise, most automobiles were manufactured in the United States, so Cuban motorists were forced to make do with old cars, for which it became increasingly difficult to obtain spare parts. For years the Cuban Sugar Kings baseball team had played in the AAA International League. Because of the embargo, league officials moved the franchise from Havana to Jersey City, New Jersey, thus depriving Cubans, who enjoy baseball just as much as Americans do, of their only professional team. Perhaps worst of all, the embargo prevented Cuba from importing food from the United States, a necessity since Cuban agriculture produced mostly sugar and tobacco. This forced the Cubans to readjust their agricultural priorities, but before that could happen it became necessary for the Castro regime to ration food.

The U.S. trade embargo made Cuba more dependent on the Soviet Union than it had ever been on the United States. This dependence contributed in part to Cuba's political evolution. Before the revolution Castro had been a lukewarm Socialist; indeed, in its early days the revolution was remarkably nonideological. But in 1961 Castro declared himself to be a Marxist-Leninist, renamed the union of the Popular Socialist Party, the March 13th Revolutionary Directorate, and the July 26th Movement the Communist Party of Cuba, and began to take Cuba down the road to communism.

Agriculture over Industry

Like most Communist nations Cuba set out to build up its industry. In 1959 what little industry Cuba had was mostly related to mining and sugar production. At first Castro worked to redirect resources into building factories that could manufacture the finished goods Cubans needed. However, by the mid-1960s he realized that industrializing Cuba was a far more daunting task than he had realized. Moreover, by this point Cuba had become so dependent on selling sugar in order to obtain the machinery, spare parts, and petroleum products it needed that it just made sense to focus on promoting agriculture rather than industry. For the remainder of Castro's regime the Cuban government devoted much time and attention to producing agricultural technicians and developing the types of industry on which agriculture depended. Unlike Soviet communism, which subordinated agriculture to industry, the Castro regime subordinated industry to agriculture.

The Bay of Pigs Invasion

As it became more closely allied with the Soviet Union, Cuba became a focal point of the Cold War. The Cold War got hot in Cuba in 1961, when the United States backed a paramilitary invasion of Cuba. The invaders were Cuban expatriates who had been armed, equipped, and trained by the U.S. Cen-

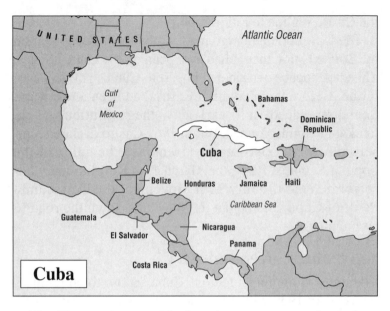

Cuba

tral Intelligence Agency. The invasion was supposed to induce the Cuban people to rise up against Castro, but as historian John C. Chasteen notes, "despite their hopes, the anti-Castro Cubans who landed at the Bay of Pigs in 1961 sparked no internal rebellion."[4] Instead, the invasion bogged down on the beaches of Playa Girón on the Bay of Pigs. After three days of intense fighting, the invaders, who were promised U.S. air support but never received it, were driven off the island by the Cuban military. In addition to embarrassing the United States, the Cuban victory at Playa Girón made Castro a hero in the eyes of most Cubans. Rather than supplant *El Líder* (one of Castro's titles, meaning "the leader") the Bay of Pigs invasion served only to entrench him at home and boost his image, and that of communism, among the third world nations.

In 1962 the Organization of American States expelled Cuba as a member, and most OAS members withdrew their recognition of Castro's regime. This happened partly because of U.S. pressure and partly because Cuba had tried to foment armed Socialist rebellion in Venezuela, Bolivia, and the Dominican Republic. The United States also began urging OAS members to discontinue trade with Cuba, and by 1964 every OAS member except Mexico had done so. Isolated even further from its natural trading partners, Cuba turned increasingly to the Soviet Union for assistance.

In 1975 the OAS ended its political and economic sanctions against Cuba, thus making it possible for Cuba to begin trading once again with its Latin American neighbors. Although these nations had never traded extensively with Cuba, they now constituted a major source of non-Soviet trade, which Cuba welcomed. Despite the end of OAS sanctions the United States remained committed to its trade embargo against Cuba, largely because it did not want to contribute to the support of a Communist regime just ninety miles from its shores. Nevertheless, the Cuban economy remained highly dependent on Soviet trade and subsidies.

The Cuban Missile Crisis

The Soviets willingly responded to Castro's request for economic aid, but at a price. The United States had deployed nuclear missiles in Turkey not far from its border with the Soviet Union, and the Soviets now suggested to Castro that they be allowed to deploy similar missiles in Cuba. Castro agreed. When the United States found out about the missiles, it blockaded the island and forced a showdown with the Soviets that almost resulted in World War III. Fortunately, nuclear Armageddon was avoided when both sides agreed to remove their missiles.

As part of the agreement the United States promised (although it never publicly acknowledged the promise) to respect the legitimacy of Castro's regime and refrain from further invasions of the island. Once again Castro had won an impressive victory against the United States, and his stature among Cubans approached that of a demigod. But despite the agreement the Playa Girón invasion and the Cuban missile crisis convinced Castro that the United States would never rest until his regime had been eliminated. He set out to repress any and all anti-Communist sentiment in Cuba and to minimize U.S. influence on the Cuban media. According to Robert E. Quirk, a Castro biographer, *El Líder*'s list of enemies included

counterrevolutionaries, imperialists, American marines, Bay of

Pigs "mercenaries," Latin American populist democrats, "bandits" fighting in the Escambray [mountains], Catholic priests, Seventh-Day Adventists, Jehovah's Witnesses, Pentacostalists, Gideonites, bureaucrats, lumpen, worms [Cuban expatriates living in the United States], slackers, and black-market profiteers.[5]

To defend Cuba against its enemies Castro set about building up Cuba's armed forces. As Orlando Castro Hidalgo has noted, "The Soviet Union provided Cuba with most of its military equipment, and this has made the Cuban Army the most powerful in Latin America."[6] In part, the Cuban armed forces were intended to assist violent Communist rebellion throughout Latin America, and they played a significant role in winning victories for pro-Communist movements in Angola and Ethiopia as well. But part of the growth of the Cuban military was to resist the next U.S. invasion of the island, which Castro was sure would eventually come.

Building Socialism in Cuba

In addition to dealing with the embargo and the Cold War, Castro's regime was faced with the daunting task of building a Socialist society. Like Lenin in the early days of Soviet communism, Castro set out to create a "new man" in Cuba. His new man would eschew material incentives for working and instead labor for the moral incentives, such as the joys of doing a good job and contributing to the betterment of society. Like his archenemy U.S. president John F. Kennedy, Castro exhorted his fellow countrymen to ask what they could do for their country, not vice versa.

Schools helped create the "new man" by training children in Socialist theory and by addressing long-standing problems of sexism and racism. College admissions were opened to anyone who demonstrated an aptitude to learn, including Afro-Cubans and women, and soon Cuban universities were turning out large numbers of medical doctors, teachers, and engineers. By 1970 these new professionals, in the sense not only that they had been recently trained but also that they had been politicized, had replaced the émigrés.

As a result of these initiatives life in Cuba began to change for the better, at least for the masses. Medical care improved dramatically, and the government was able to provide every Cuban, regardless of income level, with free medical treatment. By 1987 the infant mortality rate had dropped to the point that it was the lowest in Latin America and lower than in the United States. Meanwhile, the life expectancy of a Cuban had risen from the mid-50s in 1959 to 75.4 years, the highest in Latin America.

Teachers began pouring into rural communities, and in time Cuba attained one of the highest literacy rates in North and South America. At the same time, engineers and technicians were addressing successfully many of the problems posed by the need to industrialize, while agricultural specialists were experimenting with ways to increase the productivity of Cuban agriculture.

Building Consensus, Quashing Dissent

To prevent backsliding among those who might not have embraced the revolution wholeheartedly, Committees for the Defense of the Revolution were formed all across the island. Composed of average Cubans, these neighborhood watchdog groups were entrusted with the mission of monitoring the attitudes and behaviors of the Cuban people. In this sense they were similar to the committees formed by American patriots during the Stamp Act crisis and the American Revolution to ensure the loyalty of the general population to American political ideals.

The Federation of Cuban Women was founded as a means of involving women more fully in the revolution, and the Brigades of Militant Mothers for Education encouraged women to go to work outside the home. In 1976 the Family Code went into effect; its purpose was to make it easier for women to work by encouraging gender equality and by providing more nurseries and day care facilities for the children of working women. By 1992 women constituted more than 60 percent of the middle- and upper-level technicians, 50 percent of the medical doctors, and 40 percent of the health and education executives.

To boost productivity, various awards and medals were given to workers who produced over and above what was expected of them. A major source of moral incentive was the oratory of Castro himself, who continuously reminded Cubans of the external threat posed by the United States and of the need to work hard to negate that threat.

Like the Soviets, Castro also worked to diminish the influence of religion in Cuba. Communists have generally regarded organized religion as an alternative source of authority to the state, especially since most religions have condemned communism. The Roman Catholic Church was particularly repugnant to Castro because it drew its greatest support from the wealthy and professional classes, the natural enemies of the revolution. But unlike the Soviets, the Castro regime was unable to stamp out religious worship completely. For a while the regime managed to shut down the Roman Catholic churches and run out most of the priests and nuns, thus preventing devout Cubans from attending weekly mass. However, the church continued to maintain a presence despite the persecutions.

By 1985 the Castro regime realized that communism and Catholicism were not necessarily antithetical. As Castro himself admitted, "Christianity has utopian elements too, just as socialism and communism have."[7] The regime also realized that many Cubans who wanted sincerely to be good Communists were put off by religious persecutions. That same year the Cuban government opened the Office for Religious Affairs, which was intended to foster a better relationship between the church and the state. By the late 1990s the Roman Catholic Church in Cuba included thirteen bishops and almost three hundred priests, all of them operating openly. The church received a real boost in 1998, when Pope John Paul II visited Cuba, and as a result the future of Cuban Catholicism seems to be more secure.

The Castro regime also became more accepting of the various Afro-Cuban religions. The most popular is Santería, which combines features of African worship with certain aspects of Roman Catholicism, particularly its emphasis on the saints. Since 1985 Santeria devotees have been able to worship the *orishas*, or gods, more or less openly.

The Revolution's First Thirty Years

Between 1959 and 1989 the Castro regime made tremendous progress toward reforming Cuban society. The upper and middle classes had been virtually eliminated, mostly via emigration, and the working class had risen up to a new position of importance. Cubans enjoyed universal schooling and health care and improved housing, and the deleterious effects of racism and sexism were being addressed if not altogether eliminated.

On the downside, the Cuban economy had not really grown; communism merely redistributed wealth without creating new wealth. The totalitarian nature of the Castro regime stifled internal political debate and outlawed the expression of any political theory or opinion that contradicted socialism, although in this sense it was not very different from the pro-U.S. regimes it had replaced. Beset by massive opposition from the United States and its allies and growing dissension on the island, the regime bolstered the Cuban military and turned Cuba into what several scholars have called a garrison state. In assessing the first quarter-century of the revolution, Hugh S. Thomas, Georges A. Fauriol, and Juan Carlos Weiss say of Castro's regime, "Its principal features include the militarization of society; the government monopolization of public opinion and all social, economic, and political activity; mass radicalization; and the idea of constant warfare against both internal and external enemies."[8]

The Dawn of the Special Period

The collapse of European communism beginning in 1989 created many new difficulties for Castro's Cuba. According to historian Max Azicri, "the collapse of European socialism confronted the Cuban regime with a survival crisis."[9] Despite having renewed economic ties with Latin America, more than 85 percent of Cuba's foreign trade was with Communist-bloc nations. When their governments began to embrace free markets, Cubans were forced to rework almost all of their existing trade agreements. The Soviet Union had been the world's largest consumer of sugar, and when it broke apart in 1991 Cuba lost its best customer, not to mention its primary supplier of machinery, spare parts, petroleum, and grain. Ever since, the Castro regime has scrambled to find new customers for Cuban sugar and new suppliers of manufactured goods and oil, but so far it has failed to find enough of either. Cubans faced so many new problems that the era after 1989 became known as the Special Period, a time of hardships without war.

The Castro regime's first measure was belt tightening. Food and fuel were rationed more strictly than before, and electricity was cut off for as much as seven hours a day. Since the government's income had been sharply reduced by the decline of sugar sales, volunteer work brigades were encouraged to take up the many work projects that remained uncompleted, in much the same way that Americans are encouraged to build homes for their less fortunate neighbors by participating in Habitat for Humanity. The production of sugar itself was reduced by almost half, and millions of acres of sugarcane were given over instead to the raising of vegetables and cattle. Because maximum loyalty to the regime was required in order to weather the Special Period, military officers were put in charge of an increasing number of civilian organizations and businesses.

The Return of Tourism

During the Special Period it became imperative to find new ways to replace the income and the subsidies Cuba had received from trade with the Soviet bloc. One answer was to encourage tourism. Castro had never prevented Cubans from leaving the island; what held up their departure was the refusal of other countries, including the United States, to grant visas. But foreign visitors to Cuba had been greatly restricted, mostly because of the threat of U.S.-backed terrorism (in 1975 the CIA admitted publicly that it had tried to assassinate Castro on eight different occasions).

In 1989 the doors of Cuba were thrown open to foreigners. New hotels and restaurants were constructed, beaches were cleaned up, and retail stores featuring quality merchandise at reasonable prices were opened near likely tourist attractions. All of these establishments took only foreign currency, especially U.S. dollars, and barred Cubans as customers.

One result of the return of tourism was an influx of much-needed foreign currency with which to buy imported food and machinery. Another was to disillusion many Cubans, particularly young ones, with communism, which suddenly seemed unable to provide the material goods that they wanted but that foreign capitalists possessed in abundance. A third was a spate of terrorist attacks in 1997 on tourist hotels by U.S.-based Cuban expatriates.

The growing tourism industry required large numbers of service personnel, including wait staff, baggage handlers, guides, and entertainers, and many Cubans began entering these career paths. Ironically, because they came into contact with foreigners on a regular basis, they acquired foreign currency more readily than did other Cubans. The currency and the contacts gave them access to consumer goods that were beyond the means of medical doctors, business managers, and other professionals.

Tourism also gave rise to a thriving unofficial service industry and blurred the distinctions between the official economy and the black market. *Jineteros* and *jineteras*, black market hustlers and prostitutes, crowded the streets of Old Havana and other places that were popular with tourists. The Castro regime, which had prided itself on getting rid of prostitution in the 1960s, reluctantly tolerated such business practices.

Cuba Moves Toward a Market Economy

Tourism helped ease Cuba's economic woes, but by no means did it solve them all. In 1993 Castro reluctantly allowed Cubans to open their own small businesses. Shops and street vendors, peddling a wide range of goods and services at free-market prices, began catering to Cubans. The government profited from this entrepreneurial activity via licenses and income taxes, the first imposed on Cubans since 1959.

In 1993 the *granjas*, or state-run farms, were replaced with Basic Units of Cooperative Production (UBPCs), in essence worker-managed cooperative farms. UBPCs were given greater control over their enterprise, including the right to produce what they wished and to own what they produced. Although worker satisfaction seems to have increased as workers gain greater control over their own workplace, the overall productivity of the UBPCs did not increase much due to shortages of fuel, fertilizer, and pesticides, all of which had been obtained from the Soviet Union.

Another economic reform pushed by Castro during the Special Period was to permit foreign corporations to enter into joint ventures with the Cuban government. Several corporations, mostly headquartered in western Europe and Canada, responded to this overture. Largely as a result, Cuba was able to trade fish for Spanish manufactured goods, nickel for Canadian wheat, fruit for German machinery, and sugar for Japanese machinery. A number of joint ventures involved biotechnology; denied direct access to pharmaceuticals by the U.S. trade embargo, Cuban medical research had focused on developing medicines and drugs, and the results were sophisticated and astonishing.

Castro's Legacy

As of 2003 Fidel Castro was still *El Líder*, a position he had held since 1959. Critics blast him for oppressing the Cuban people, specifically for refusing to allow meaningful elections to take place and for denying Cuban dissidents the right to speak out against his regime. As Tony Mendoza noted after a 1997 visit to Havana, "every Cuban I talked to was very clear about this: if you are vocal in your opposition to the regime, you end up in jail."[10] Critics also lambaste Cuban communism because it has not created new wealth but merely redistributed existing wealth, and because the collapse of European communism "proves" that communism in general does not work. They dismiss Castro as being irrelevant, and call for his resignation so that a new leader can move Cuba forward into the modern age of free elections and free markets.

Supporters praise Castro for improving the standard of living of the average Cuban, at least in the thirty years before the Special Period. They also applaud him for being flexible enough ideologically to move Cuban socialism toward a mixed economy that hopefully will eventually incorporate the best features of communism and capitalism.

In fact, it is quite difficult to assess Castro's impact on Cuba from the perspective of "good" and "evil." No one can deny that under Castro and during the heyday of Soviet communism, life for the Cuban masses improved dramatically. Likewise, no one can deny that much of the cost for this improvement was paid by the island's wealthy and professional classes, many of whom fled the island and bitterly detest Castro to this day. And it is true that in many respects life in Cuba during the Special Period seems to be returning to its prerevolutionary state. Whether Castro's regime can weather the storm and revitalize Cuban communism, or whether it will dissipate with Castro's death or political demise, remains to be seen.

Notes

1. Louis A. Pérez Jr., *On Becoming Cuban: Identity, Nationality, and Culture.* Chapel Hill: University of North Carolina Press, 1999, p. 469.
2. Jaime Suchlicki, *Cuba: From Columbus to Castro and Beyond*, 4th ed. Washington, DC: Brassey's, 1997, p. 155.
3. Jesús Arboleya, *The Cuban Counterrevolution.* Athens, OH: University Center for International Studies, 2000, p. 45.
4. John C. Chasteen, *Born in Blood and Fire: A Concise History of Latin America.* New York: W.W. Norton, 2001, p. 265.
5. Robert E. Quirk, *Fidel Castro: The Full Story of His Rise to Power, His Regime, His Allies, and His Adversaries.* New York: W.W. Norton, 1993, p. 525.
6. Orlando Castro Hidalgo, *Spy for Fidel.* Miami: E.A. Seemann, 1971, p. 63.
7. Quoted in Frei Betto, *Fidel and Religion: Castro Talks on Revolu-*

tion and Religion with Frei Betto. New York: Simon and Schuster, 1987, p. 221.

8. Hugh S. Thomas, Georges A. Fauriol, and Juan Carlos Weiss, *The Cuban Revolution: Twenty-Five Years Later.* Boulder, CO: Westview, 1984, p. 18.

9. Max Azicri, *Cuba Today and Tomorrow: Reinventing Socialism.* Gainesville: University Press of Florida, 2000, p. 277.

10. Tony Mendoza, *Cuba—Going Back.* Austin: University of Texas Press, 1997, p. 99.

Chapter 1

Castro Takes Command

Chapter Preface

When Fidel Castro led the attack on Moncada army barracks on July 26, 1953, he had no intention of turning Cuba into a Socialist state, or even of becoming its leader. Like many other Cubans, he simply wanted to restore the constitution of 1940. The constitution promised to make life more equitable for the average Cuban via political and economic reform, but it, and the reforms, had been suspended by Fulgencio Batista in 1952. After taking power in 1959, however, Castro became convinced that social reform of the magnitude required to transform Cuba was not possible through capitalism, and he began to lead his country down the socialist road.

As in most countries that embraced socialism, most Cubans, especially the poor ones, had no interest in socialism or any other political theory. What they were interested in was food, shelter, clothing, education, and health care. When Castro promised to deliver these things, they followed him hopefully. And the vast majority of them continued to follow him for decades, even when the promise of socialism began to fade. This phenomenon can be explained in two ways: repressive security measures within Cuba and Castro's incredibly charismatic personality. When Castro spoke in public, which was often in the early days, he enthralled his listeners with his magnificent oratory. He also displayed a great deal of compassion for the typical Cuban, the one who had been mired in poverty in prerevolutionary times.

Not all Cubans embraced Castro or his reforms. Many, particularly the upper and middle classes, fled Cuba because they knew that socialism would make their lives more difficult, not better. Others plotted against the Castro regime, but they were arrested, tried, and imprisoned, oftentimes in unspeakably harsh conditions.

The Ideology of the Early Revolution

Fidel Castro

When Fidel Castro first set out to take control of Cuba, he was not a Communist or even a socialist. Instead, like many Cubans, he simply wanted to rid Cuba of its corrupt and repressive leader, Fulgencio Batista, and create a society that served the people of Cuba, not foreign investors. To this end, he espoused land reform, improved education and health care, industrialization, profit sharing, and political and civil liberties. Many of these reforms were addressed in the Cuban Constitution of 1940, but Batista suspended that in 1952.

On July 26, 1953, Castro led a failed assault on the Moncada military barracks in Santiago de Cuba. He was arrested by the Batista government, tried, and sentenced to prison. This excerpt is taken from his defense plea (Castro, a trained lawyer, spoke for himself) during his trial. It outlines his political agenda at that time and identifies the constituency for whom he fights. Convinced that his views were correct and that his methods would eventually succeed, the plea ends: "Sentence me. I don't mind. History will absolve me."

Following the overthrow of Batista in 1959, Castro claimed that the revolution was not red, the color of socialism, but olive green, the color of the rebel troops' fatigues. That same year, however, he began to implement certain socialist reforms such as collective farming, and in 1961 he proclaimed the revolution to be a socialist cause. Following the abortive invasion by U.S.-backed Cuban expatriates at Playa Girón in 1961, Castro publicly announced himself to be a Marxist-Leninist.

Fidel Castro, *History Will Absolve Me*. Secaucus, NJ: Lyle Stuart, 1961.

I stated that the second consideration on which we based our chances for success was one of social order because we were assured of the people's support. When we speak of the people we do not mean the comfortable ones, the conservative elements of the nation, who welcome any regime of oppression, any dictatorship, any despotism, prostrating themselves before the master of the moment until they grind their foreheads into the ground. When we speak of struggle, the *people* means the vast unredeemed masses, to whom all make promises and whom all deceive; we mean the people who yearn for a better, more dignified and more just nation; who are moved by ancestral aspirations of justice, for they have suffered injustice and mockery, generation after generation; who long for great and wise changes in all aspects of their life; people, who, to attain these changes, are ready to give even the very last breath of their lives—when they believe in something or in someone, especially when they believe in themselves. In stating a purpose, the first condition of sincerity and good faith, is to do precisely what nobody else ever does, that is, to speak with absolute clarity, without fear. The demagogues and professional politicians who manage to perform the miracle of being right in everything and in pleasing everyone, are, of necessity, deceiving everyone about everything. The revolutionaries must proclaim their ideas courageously, define their principles and express their intentions so that no one is deceived, neither friend nor foe.

Castro's Constituency

The people we counted on in our struggle were these:

Seven hundred thousand Cubans without work, who desire to earn their daily bread honestly without having to emigrate in search of livelihood.

Five hundred thousand farm laborers inhabiting miserable shacks, who work four months of the year and starve for the rest of the year, sharing their misery with their children, who have not an inch of land to cultivate, and whose existence inspires compassion in any heart not made of stone.

Four hundred thousand industrial laborers and stevedores whose retirement funds have been embezzled, whose benefits are being taken away, whose homes are wretched quarters, whose salaries pass from the hands of the boss to those of the usurer, whose future is a pay reduction and dismissal, whose life is eternal work and whose only rest is in the tomb.

One hundred thousand small farmers who live and die working on land that is not theirs, looking at it with sadness as Moses did the promised land, to die without possessing it; who, like feudal serfs, have to pay for the use of their parcel of land by giving up a portion of their products; who cannot love it, improve it, beautify it or plant a lemon or an orange tree on it, because they never know when a sheriff will come with the rural guard to evict them from it.

Thirty thousand teachers and professors who are so devoted, dedicated and necessary to the better destiny of future generations and who are so badly treated and paid.

Twenty thousand small businessmen weighted down by debts, ruined by the crisis and harangued by a plague of filibusters and venal officials.

Ten thousand young professionals: doctors, engineers, lawyers, veterinarians, school teachers, dentists, pharmacists, newspapermen, painters, sculptors, etc., who come forth from school with their degrees, anxious to work and full of hope, only to find themselves at a dead end with all doors closed, and where no ear hears their clamor or supplication.

These are the people, the ones who know misfortune and, therefore, are capable of fighting with limitless courage!

To the people whose desperate roads through life have been paved with the brick of betrayals and false promises, we were not going to say: "we will eventually give you what you need, but rather—Here you have it, fight for it with all your might so that liberty and happiness may be yours!"

The Five Revolutionary Laws

In the brief of this cause there must be recorded the five revolutionary laws that would have been proclaimed immediately after the capture of the Moncada barracks and would have been broadcast to the nation by radio. It is possible that Colonel Chaviano[1] may deliberately have destroyed these documents, but even if he has done so, I conserve them in my memory.

The First Revolutionary Law would have returned power to the people and proclaimed the Constitution of 1940 the supreme Law of the land, until such time as the people should decide to modify or change it. And, in order to effect its implementation and punish those who had violated it—there being no organization for holding elections to accomplish this—the revolutionary movement, as the momentous incarnation of this sovereignty, the only source of legitimate power, would have assumed all the faculties inherent to it, except that of modifying the Constitution itself: In other words it would have assumed the legislative, executive and judicial powers.

This approach could not be more crystal clear nor more free of vacillation and sterile charlatanry. A government acclaimed by the mass of rebel people would be vested with every power, everything necessary in order to proceed with the effective implementation of the popular will and true justice. From that moment, the Judicial Power, which since March 10th has placed itself *against* the Constitution and *outside* the Constitution, would cease to exist and we would proceed to its immediate and total reform before it would again assume the power granted to it by the Supreme Law of the Republic. Without our first taking those previous measures, a return to legality by putting the custody of the courts back into the hands that have crippled the system so dishonorably would constitute a fraud, a deceit, and one more betrayal.

The Second Revolutionary Law would have granted property, not mortgageable and not transferable, to all planters, sub-planters, lessees, partners and squatters who hold parcels of five or less "caballerias" [i.e., no more than 160 acres] of land, and the state would indemnify the former

---

1. Colonel Alberto del Rio Chaviano was the chief of Oriente Province when Castro's men attacked Moncada barracks.

owners on the basis of the rental which they would have received for these parcels over a period of ten years.

The Third Revolutionary Law would have granted workers and employees the right to share 30% of the profits of all the large industrial, mercantile and mining enterprises, including the sugar mills. The strictly agricultural enterprises would be exempt in consideration of other agrarian laws which would have been implemented.

The Fourth Revolutionary Law would have granted all planters the right to share 55% of the sugar production and a minimum quota of forty thousand "arrobas"[2] for all small planters who have been established for three or more years.

The Fifth Revolutionary Law would have ordered the confiscation of all holdings and ill-gotten gains of those who had committed frauds during previous regimes, as well as the holdings and ill-gotten gains of all their legatees and heirs. To implement this, special courts with full powers would gain access to all records of all corporations registered or operating in this country [in order] to investigate concealed funds of illegal origin, and to request that foreign governments extradite persons and attach holdings [rightfully belonging to the Cuban people]. Half of the property recovered would be used to subsidize retirement funds for workers and the other half would be used for hospitals, asylums and charitable organizations.

Furthermore, it was to be declared that the Cuban policy in the Americas would be one of close solidarity with the democratic people of this continent, and that those politically persecuted by bloody tyrants oppressing our sister nations would find generous asylum, brotherhood, and bread in the land of Martí.[3] Not the persecution, hunger and treason that they find today. Cuba should be the bulwark of liberty and not a shameful link in the chain of despotism.

These laws would have been proclaimed immediately, as soon as the upheaval were ended and prior to a detailed and

2. Forty thousand arrobas is roughly equivalent to five hundred tons.   3. José Martí (1853–1895) was a Cuban poet who symbolized Cuba's struggle for independence from Spain.

far-reaching study, they would have been followed by another series of laws and fundamental measures, such as, the Agrarian Reform, Integral Reform of Education, nationalization of the Utilities Trust and the Telephone Trust, refund to the people of the illegal excessive rates this company has charged, and payment to the Treasury of all taxes brazenly evaded in the past.

All these laws and others would be inspired in the exact fulfillment of two essential articles of our Constitution. One of these orders the outlawing of feudal estates by indicating the maximum area of land any person or entity can possess for each type of agricultural enterprise, by adopting measures which would tend to revert the land to the Cubans. The other categorically orders the State to use all means at its disposal to provide employment to all those who lack it and to insure a decent livelihood to each manual laborer or intellectual.

None of these articles may be called unconstitutional. The first popularly elected government would have to respect these laws, not only because of moral obligation to the nation, but because when people achieve something they have yearned for throughout generations, no force in the world is capable of taking it away again.

The problems concerning land, the problem of industrialization, the problem of housing, the problem of unemployment, the problem of education and the problem of the health of the people; these are the six problems we would take immediate steps to resolve, along with the restoration of public liberties and political democracy.

Perhaps this exposition appears cold and theoretical if one does not know the shocking and tragic conditions of the country with regard to these six problems, to say nothing of the most humiliating political oppression.

Land and Industrialization

85% of the small farmers in Cuba pay rent and live under the constant threat of being dispossessed from the land that they cultivate. More than half the best cultivated land belongs to foreigners. In *Oriente*, the largest province, the lands of the

United Fruit Company and West Indian Company join the north coast to the southern one. There are two hundred thousand peasant families who do not have a single acre of land to cultivate to provide food for their starving children. On the other hand, nearly three hundred thousand "caballerias" [i.e., almost 10 million acres] of productive land owned by powerful interests remains uncultivated.

Fidel Castro

Cuba is above all an agricultural state. Its population is largely rural. The city depends on these rural areas. The rural people won the Independence. The greatness and prosperity of our country depends on a healthy and vigorous rural population that loves the land and knows how to cultivate it, within the framework of a state that protects and guides them. Considering all this, how can the present state of affairs be tolerated any longer?

With the exception of a few food, lumber and textile industries, Cuba continues to be a producer of raw materials. We export sugar to import candy, we export hides to import shoes, we export iron to import plows. Everybody agrees that the need to industrialize the country is urgent, that we need steel industries, paper and chemical industries; that we must improve cattle and grain products, the technique and the processing in our food industry, in order to balance the ruinous competition of the Europeans in cheese products, condensed milk, liquors and oil, and that of the Americans in canned goods; that we need merchant ships; that tourism should be an enormous source of revenue. . . .

Housing and Education

Just as serious or even worse is the housing problem. There are two hundred thousand huts and hovels in Cuba; four hundred thousand families in the country and in the cities live cramped into barracks and tenements without even the minimum sanitary requirements; two million two hundred thousand of our urban population pay rents which absorb between one fifth and one third of their income; and two million eight hundred thousand of our rural and suburban population lack electricity. If the State proposes lowering rents, landlords threaten to freeze all construction; if the State does not interfere, construction goes on so long as the landlords get high rents, otherwise, they would not lay a single brick even though the rest of the population should have to live exposed to the elements. The utilities monopoly is no better: they extend lines as far as it is profitable and beyond that point, they don't care if the people have to live in darkness for the rest of their lives. The State folds its arms and the people have neither homes nor electricity.

Our educational system is perfectly compatible with the rest of our national situation. Where the *guajiro* [small farmer] is not the owner of his land, what need is there for agricultural schools? Where there are no industries what need is there for technical or industrial schools? Everything falls within the same absurd logic: there is neither one thing nor the other. In any small European country there are more than 200 technical and industrial arts schools; in Cuba, there are only six such schools, and the boys graduate without having anywhere to use their skills. The little rural schools are attended by only half the school-age children—barefoot, half-naked and undernourished—and frequently the teacher must buy necessary materials from his own salary. Is this the way to make a nation great?

Health and Unemployment

Only death can liberate one from so much misery. In this, however,—early death—the state is most helpful. 90% of rural children are consumed by parasites which filter through their bare feet from the earth. Society is moved to compassion upon hearing of the kidnapping or murder of one child, but they are criminally indifferent to the mass murder of so many thousands of children who die every year from lack of facilities, agonizing with pain. Their innocent eyes—death already shining in them—seem to look into infinity as if entreating forgiveness for human selfishness, as if asking God to stay his wrath. When the head of a family works only four months a year, with what can he purchase clothing and medicine for his children? They will grow up with rickets, with not a single good tooth in their mouths by the time they reach thirty; they will have heard ten million speeches and will finally die of misery and deception. Public hospitals, which are always full, accept only patients recommended by some powerful politician who, in turn, demands the electoral votes of the unfortunate one and his family so that Cuba may continue forever the same or worse.

With this background, is it not understandable that from May to December over a million persons lost their jobs, and that Cuba, with a population of five and a half million, has a greater percentage of unemployed than France or Italy with a population of forty million each?

When you judge a defendant for robbery, Your Honors, do you ask him how long he has been unemployed? Do you ask him how many children he has, which days of the week he ate and which he didn't, do you concern yourselves with his environment at all? You send him to jail without further thought. But those who burn warehouses and stores to collect insurance do not go to jail. . . . The insured have money to hire lawyers and bribe judges. You jail the poor wretch who steals because he is hungry; but none of the hundreds who steal from the Government has ever spent a night in jail; you dine with them at the end of the year in some elegant place and they enjoy your respect. . . .

The future of the country and the solution of its problems cannot continue to depend on the selfish interests of a dozen financiers, nor on the cold calculations of profits that ten or twelve magnates draw up in their air-conditioned offices. The country cannot continue begging on its knees for miracles from a few golden calves, similar to the Biblical one destroyed by the fury of a prophet. Golden calves cannot perform miracles of any kind. The problems of the Republic can be solved only if we dedicate ourselves to fight for that Republic with the same energy, honesty and patriotism our liberators had when they created it.

Solving the Six Problems

It is not by statesmen such as Carlos Saladrigas [a puppet of Batista], whose statesmanship consists of preserving the status quo and mouthing phrases like the "absolute freedom of enterprise," "guarantees to investment capital" and "the law of supply and demand," that we will solve these problems. Those ministers can chat gaily in a mansion on Fifth Avenue [a fashionable residential street in Havana] until there remains not even the dust of the bones of those whose problems required immediate solution. In this present-day world, social problems are not solved by spontaneous generation.

A revolutionary government with the backing of the people and the respect of the nation, after cleaning the various institutions of all venal and corrupt officials, would proceed immediately to industrialize the country, mobilizing all inactive capital, currently estimated at about 500 million dollars, through the National Bank and the Agricultural, Industrial and Development Bank, and submitting this mammoth task to experts and men of absolute competence, completely removed from all political machinations, for study, direction, planning and realization.

After settling the one hundred thousand small farmers as owners on land which they previously rented, a revolutionary government would proceed immediately to settle the land problem. First, as the Constitution orders we would establish the maximum amount of land to be held by each type of agricultural enterprise and would acquire the excess acres by: expropriation, recovery of the lands stolen from the State, improvement of swampland, planting of large nurseries and reserving of zones for reforestation. Secondly, we would distribute the remaining land among peasant families with priority given to the larger ones, and would promote agricultural cooperatives with a single technical, professional direction in farming and cattle raising. Finally, we would provide resources, equipment, protection and useful guidance to the peasants.

A revolutionary government would solve the housing problem by cutting all rents in half, by providing tax exemptions on homes inhabited by the owners; by tripling taxes on rented homes; by tearing down hovels and replacing them with modern multiple-dwelling buildings; and by financing housing all over the island on a scale heretofore unheard of; with the criterion that, just as each rural family should possess its own tract of land, each city family should own its home or apartment. There is plenty of building material and more than enough manpower to make a decent home for every Cuban. But if we continue to wait for the miracle of the golden calf, a thousand years will have gone by and the problem will still be the same. On the other hand, today there are greater than ever possibilities of bringing electricity to the remotest corner of the island. The use of nuclear energy in this field is now a reality and will greatly reduce the cost of producing electricity.

With these three projects and reforms, the problem of unemployment would automatically disappear and the work to improve public health and to fight against disease would be made much less difficult.

Finally, a revolutionary government would undertake the integral reform of the educational system, bringing it in line with the foregoing projects with the idea of educating those generations who will have the privilege of living in a happy land. Do not forget the words of the Apóstol [José Martí]: "A serious error is being made in Latin America: where the inhabitants depend almost exclusively on the products of the soil for their livelihood, the education stress, contradictorally, is on urban rather than farm life." "The happiest people are the ones whose children are well-educated and instructed in philosophy; whose sentiments are directed into noble channels." "A well-educated people will always be strong and free."

The spirit of education lies, however, in the teacher him-

self and in Cuba the teaching profession is miserably un-
derpaid. Despite this, no one is more dedicated than the
Cuban teacher. Who among us has not learned his ABC's in
the little public schoolhouse? It is time we stopped paying
pittances to these young men and women who are entrusted
with the sacred task of teaching the young. No teacher
should earn less than $200, no secondary professor should
get less than $350, if they are to devote themselves exclu-
sively to their high calling without suffering want. Moreover, all rural teachers should have free use of the various
systems of transportation; and, at least every five years, all
teachers should enjoy a sabbatical leave of six months with
pay so they may attend special refresher courses at home
and abroad to keep abreast of the latest developments in
their field. In this way, the curriculum and the teaching system may be constantly improved.

Where will the money be found for all this? When there
is an end to rife embezzlement of government funds, when
public officials stop taking graft from the large companies
who owe taxes to the State, when the enormous resources
of the country are brought into full use, when we no longer
buy tanks, bombers and guns for this country (which has no
frontiers to defend and where these instruments of war, now
being purchased, are used against the people) when there is
more interest in educating the people than in killing them—
then there will be more than enough money.

For a Better Cuba

Cuba could easily provide for a population three times as
great as it now has, so there is no excuse for the abject
poverty of a single one of its present inhabitants. The markets should be overflowing with produce, pantries should be
full, all hands should be working. This is not an inconceivable thought. What is inconceivable is that anyone should
go to bed hungry, that children should die for lack of medical attention; what is inconceivable is that 30% of our farm
people cannot write their names and that 99% of them know
nothing of Cuba's history. What is inconceivable is that the

majority of our rural people are now living in worse circumstances than were the Indians Columbus discovered living in the fairest land that human eyes had ever seen.

To those who would call me a dreamer, I quote the words of Martí: "A true man does not seek the path where advantage lies, but rather, the path where duty lies, and this is the only practical man, whose dream of today will be the law of tomorrow, because he who has looked back on the upheavals of history and has seen civilizations going up in flames, crying out in bloody struggle, throughout the centuries, knows that the future well-being of man, without exception, lies on the side of duty."

Castro Enthralled Cubans with His Oratory

José Luis Llovio-Menéndez

Virtually everyone who has come into contact with Fidel Castro marvels at his profound abilities as a speaker. Trained as a lawyer, he can speak for hours with the utmost confidence on virtually any topic. Although he often goes off on tangents during his speeches, Castro almost always relates them to the main topic in such a way that illuminates rather than confuses. A number of foreign observers have remarked that most Cubans, even working-class ones, are surprisingly articulate. Some attribute this fact to Cuba's excellent education system, while others give credit to the almost-daily exposure Cubans get to Castro's oratory. Most observers agree that Castro's speaking skills are a major reason for his continued popularity with the Cuban people.

José Luis Llovio-Menéndez fought as a guerrilla in the revolution and served as a high-ranking bureaucrat in Castro's government. His disillusionment with communism, however, eventually led him to leave Cuba. In this excerpt, he describes a typical speech by Fidel Castro, this one given in 1963 on the tenth anniversary of the July 26th Movement that brought Castro to power.

On July 26, 1963, by invitation from [the secretary of the United Party of the Cuban Socialist Revolution, Emilio] Aragonés, came my first opportunity to witness one of Fidel's

José Luis Llovio-Menéndez, *Insider: My Hidden Life as a Revolutionary in Cuba*, translated by Edith Grossman. New York: Bantam Books, 1988. Copyright © 1988 by José Luis Llovio-Menéndez. All rights reserved. Reproduced by permission.

famous oratorical addresses. A party car delivered me to the Plaza two hours before Fidel was scheduled to speak. In the warm forenoon of a Cuban summer day, a large crowd had already begun to gather. All city streets that gave immediate access to the area around the Martí memorial, where Fidel would be, were manned by security guards. Only drivers in authorized vehicles who could also produce an invitation and a parking permit were allowed through. I was among them.

Castro Makes the Entrance

Minutes before the ceremony was to begin, Fidel arrived in a 1960 Oldsmobile. From my seat I noticed he was wearing a clean, pressed uniform, unusual then for the Commander-in-Chief. He stopped to talk with Interior Minister Ramiro Valdés and José Abrantes, the head of State Security. Standing nearby were Comandante Vallejo, Pepín Naranjo, and Carlos Rafael Rodríguez, the [Popular Socialist Party] (PSP) attorney and former Batista minister who had denounced the Moncada assault in 1953 [a failed attack upon a Batista barracks during which Castro was captured].

The lower part of the official platform was full of Asian, African, and European faces. On the upper rostrum, reserved for the higher echelons of the Cuban party and government, I saw Raúl Castro and Osvaldo Dorticós, President of the Republic, whose power was nominal and whose duties were largely ceremonial. Dorticós was known as *Cucharón*, the Big Spoon. He didn't cut like a knife or stab like a fork, people said. The Big Spoon was a figurehead.

The crowd had swollen to a half-million people or more now, filling the Plaza. I saw thousands of Cuban flags, hats, berets, and placards. Immense portraits of Marx, Engels, and Lenin covered the walls of the nearby buildings. Over the many loudspeakers blared patriotic and revolutionary songs.

Then the sweltering Plaza exploded into a great roar of "Fidel! Fidel! Fidel!" as he came out from the back, smiling and waving along a respectful waiting line of his highest leaders. Fidel removed his belt and pistol and sat on the left of the podium next to his brother Raúl. The crowd's thunder stopped only temporarily for the national anthem. It required Fidel himself to quiet the people long enough for him to be introduced.

This was to be a consummate performance of several hours' duration and a day of mood, not of substance. What Fidel actually said was not the point; in fact, when I later read the speech I hardly recognized the words. Throughout, I paid close attention to him from my place on the platform, about fifteen feet away. And no sooner did he begin than I felt a strange, profound sense of connection between the huge mass of people and their *Líder Máximo* [supreme leader].

Castro Mesmerizes the Crowd

Fidel stood before them, fully conscious of his magnetism. He controlled every movement and modulated his voice to perfection, manipulating the crowd as he chose.

Exporting Counterrevolution

A number of upper- and middle-class Cubans, the ones who had prospered under Fulgencio Batista's regime, refused to embrace the societal changes of the revolution. Many of these dissidents began leaving Cuba immediately after Castro came to power. Most of these expatriates settled in Florida, and provided the manpower for the failed U.S.-backed invasion at Playa Girón, or the Bay of Pigs, in 1961. Unlike other Communist regimes, Castro's did little to prevent dissidents from leaving, and even encouraged them to do so after 1966. Author Elizabeth Sutherland reported on the exodus from her 1969 book The Youngest Revolution: A Personal Report on Cuba.

For people leaving the country, [Varadero] is a final jumping-off point: two flights a day to Miami, five days a week, seventy-five to ninety persons on each flight. Under a U.S.-Cuban agreement from 1966, an American plane shuttles back and forth between the two countries, empty on the hop to Cuba and full on the way back to Florida. Before each flight from the island, a Cuban doctor of the Revolu-

He struck the manly pose, brought his hand to his beard as a sign of deep thought, turned his head to majestic profile—both sides. As he spoke, each gesture amplified his words, conveying solemnity with a wrinkled brow, anger and defiance with heaving breaths, and threats with his forefinger thrust upward to the sky.

His hands went to the bank of microphones before him. He'd utter a phrase and then pause in thought, adjusting the microphones. Another phrase, another pause.

I could *feel* him emphasize just the right word and then repeat that emphasis. Then, for dramatic effect, there would be a void, silence. That intense, brilliant gaze was directed from time to time at his entourage, seeking the approval that was never denied. Fidel accented his moments of agitation with a slight bouncing motion and an incessant movement of his right arm up and down.

---

tion stands by in case any of the emigrés gets too upset or ill; other Revolutionary Cubans serve them juice and sandwiches. The travelers wait to pass through Emigration and then U.S. Immigration.

Of those who will talk, the majority say that they are leaving to rejoin family members who have already gone. One young woman complains that she could not get her hair done the way she likes and also that she has run out of excuses for not going to cut sugarcane. They have all had a long wait, as much as two years, for Cuban and U.S. clearance and for transportation space; most of the adults lost their jobs as soon as they applied. But then, this is the first revolution to let people leave legally. (As of 1968, every able-bodied person who applied to leave had to work full-time in agricultural production while awaiting departure—or not get clearance to go. "In other words," as one observer said, "the Revolution will not simply maintain people like that; they must help produce what they eat.")

Elizabeth Sutherland, *The Youngest Revolution: A Personal Report on Cuba.* New York: Dial Press, 1969.

Minutes, hours went by with the people in a trance. After several hours Fidel closed his speech at midafternoon with the standard "*¡Patria o Muerte!*"—"Fatherland or Death!"— and then "*¡Venceremos!*"—"We shall vanquish!"

It had been a mesmerizing example of oratory. There was more shouting and applause to end the ceremony. Fidel then donned his belt and pistol, held up his arm for a few seconds of farewell, and disappeared from public view. Behind the rostrum, where cold drinks were being served, I saw several of the foreigners congratulating him effusively.

As the Plaza emptied, I lingered to chat for a while with friends. Then, with my head burning, I returned on foot to the Havana Libre, deep in reflection over what I'd just seen.

Castro Converts Cubans to Communism

The spectacle in the Plaza was palpable proof of Fidel's hold over the Cuban people. But any objective observer of the new Cuba could see that Fidel's influence went far beyond cheap demagoguery. He was polarizing the country, radically altering the very structure of its society.

Communism, so alien a notion for Cuba, was an established fact. Paranoid distrust of the United States, especially after the Bay of Pigs, flowed from Fidel into the hearts and minds of millions. With the continuing mass exodus of professionals, the wealthy, and many of the island's skilled workers, even Cuba's demography was changing.

Most startling was the change in how Cubans saw one another. Before the revolution's triumph, the blood bonds within the typical Cuban family were practically sacrosanct, a given, a matter of pride and honor. My family's special closeness may have differed somewhat in its emphasis upon shared duty and responsibility, but ours was fundamentally the traditional Cuban attitude toward one's blood relations.

Yet once I returned to Cuba, I found that Saúl Yelín, the ICAIC [Cuban Film Institute] official with whom I had spoken in Paris, had understated conditions in the new order. In Havana, I heard stories of children denouncing their parents for counterrevolutionary activity; of parents denouncing their children to neighborhood CDRs (Committees for the Defense of the Revolution), which were organized block by block as watchdogs; and of spouses denouncing spouses.

Such accusations were hailed as the purest expressions of revolutionary dedication. One example I later heard cited approvingly was that of Jaime Crombet, president of the Communist Youth League, who had denounced his own mother as a counterrevolutionary and had her jailed—a deed considered to be of high revolutionary merit.

Life in a Political Prison

John Martino

Like most revolutionary regimes, Castro's government worked assiduously to root out counterrevolutionaries and agents of countries opposed to the revolution. Thousands were incarcerated for long terms on the slightest suspicion, and many of them were guilty of nothing more than political naivete. Most were confined in rather benign conditions while they were re-educated as to the aims of the revolution, and were released when they demonstrated that they had been rehabilitated. Those who were judged to be a serious threat to Castro's regime, however, were subjected to more stringent incarceration. The worst offenders were sentenced to the Isle of Pines, the Cuban version of Alcatraz prison, where they suffered horribly.

John Martino was an American electrical engineer who did contract work for various gambling establishments in Cuba. In 1959 he unwittingly agreed to deliver a coded message to a member of the Cuban counterrevolution, and he was arrested while delivering the message. He served forty months in Cuban prisons before being released and repatriated to the United States. In this excerpt, he describes the conditions in a prison on the Isle of Pines.

The official records showed that there were only 322 prisoners on the Isle of Pines under [former Cuban dictator Fulgencio] Batista. (Under Castro, in January 1963,

John Martino with Nathaniel Weyl, *I Was Castro's Prisoner: An American Tells His Story.* New York: The Devin-Adair Company, 1963.

there would be 5,325 politicals incarcerated there.) The political prisoners were not kept in the *circulares* [general cell block], but in the "pavilions," small apartments for prisoners whose conduct was exemplary and in which the prisoners might receive their women. In addition, under the former regime, each political prisoner was entitled to his radio, newspapers and books. They were allowed to be with their women at certain times and there were doctors and medical specialists in attendance.

When Fidel Castro was Batista's prisoner on the Isle of Pines, following his ill-fated attempt to overthrow the Cuban Government on July 26, 1953, he had his own library, was given writing materials and was allowed to write subversive tracts for publication. He had his private nurse, a man named Antonio Gil, who was doing thirty years for murder. Gil has since been set free, licensed as a doctor and is today one of the medical men in attendance on Castro. In addition, Fidel Castro had been assigned a jeep and driver.

A guard who had been on the Island when Castro was confined there told me that the chief of the prison once decided to surprise Castro and had his son, Fidelito, brought out for a visit. Told that the Chief had a surprise for him, Castro appeared in his jeep.

"Here is your son," the Chief said, in the presence of the guard who told me the story.

Castro leaned down, gave Fidelito a peck on the cheek and then proceeded to complain to the Chief that newspapermen had come to see him, but had not been allowed to take pictures. All this time, he ignored the boy. When he had finished with his complaint, Castro drove away in his jeep, leaving his son behind in tears.

When he took over in Cuba, one of Castro's first acts was to order the execution of the Chief of the prison and of his four-man military escort.

Poor Sanitation and Diet

The prison today has four *circulares*, or round buildings, six stories high and of reinforced concrete. Each of these floors has ninety-three cells, built to house either one or two prisoners each. They now house three or four. Although an adequate number of toilets was originally installed, all but one to a floor have been ripped out and sent to the Soviet Union on arms ships from Russia that would otherwise be returning empty or in ballast. The result is that there is only one toilet for every 300-odd prisoners. Since the food is often rotten, a large number of the prisoners suffer from diarrhea. Waiting in line for the toilet becomes impossible and they are obliged to use the floors of the cells or corridors. With a virtual absence of paper, the men in the *circulares* live in indescribable conditions of filth.

Dr. Guillermo Ara, who was one of the four political prisoners released by Castro in the last days of 1962, a man of about six feet who shrank from 168 to 104 pounds during sixteen months, described the food there in an article in the *Diario de las Américas* for January 6, 1963. What Dr. Ara has to say is the substance of what dozens of returned wretches from the Island, men sent back to Havana because of incurable or terminal illness, reported. I quote Ara, because he is not only accurate, but eloquent:

"There one is born again every day, because the life of a prisoner is worth nothing. Every twenty-four hours brings a renewal of tension, torture and painful hunger. Dogs are privileged characters in comparison with the political prisoners of the Isle of Pines. The day of tortures begins very early— at five. At this hour, they serve every *galera* [cell] with what they call breakfast, a piece of bread with 'coffee,' which is a dark liquid that smells like anything but coffee. That is to say, dark water and bread. Milk is something to dream about. For two years, none has been served the prisoners."

Lunch and supper consist of boiled macaroni, cassava or pumpkin. This is served without any fat or salt. The pumpkins and macaroni are often spoiled and their smell makes that inescapably clear.

This diet is one of starvation. Men become emaciated to such an extent that their ribs can be seen through their skin. Strong, powerfully built men, such as some of the Cuban aviators convicted of "war crimes" on Fidel Castro's personal orders (after a previous trial in which a Rebel tribunal had acquitted them) have shrunk to walking skeletons.

In addition, the prison diet is designed to kill because it is qualitatively insufficient for human health. There are no proteins, no protective foods, no fats, no sugars, no dairy products and none of the vitamins necessary for healthy life. Because of vitamin starvation, some of the aviators I have just mentioned are slowly going blind.

There is no running water. In the morning, a water truck is brought in and each man is allowed a pint daily for drinking. For washing, they use salt water piped in from the ocean.

The Cell Blocks

This prison was never finished. Consequently, there are no cell doors. The cell structures are doughnut-like. There are no windows, but merely apertures closed with a grating of steel bars. Hence, the rain pours in. On the inside, these openings look out to a circular stairway and to a tower which rises in the center above the roof of the circulars. There are also grated openings, facing outward, away from the skin of the doughnut, but to use these is dangerous, since the guards often fire at these apertures without warning.

The prisoners are never allowed out of the *circulares* for air and exercise. During their entire period of incarceration, they are confined inside the *circulares*. The only physical movement possible for them is from cell to cell and from floor to floor within each *circular.*

There is a commissary, but, on the Island, there is nothing to buy, not even tobacco. The prisoners are allowed to write one letter a week, which must be on one side of a single sheet of paper. Mail is received on the average once every two months. *From the summer of 1962 to January 1963, the American political prisoners on the Isle of Pines were not allowed to send any mail or to receive any mail or packages.*

Visiting rules change, depending on the political situation, much as they did at La Cabaña [a prison where the author was confined previously]. However, here things are immeasurably worse and, in good times on the Island, visiting days are limited to once every three months.

There is supposed to be an infirmary on the Island, but this is a malicious joke. It resembles a *galera* at La Cabaña. This so-called hospital has no equipment at all; its doctors are the medically trained prisoners, and the only medicines available are the packages sent in by the families and friends of the political prisoners. By late 1962, these packages were regularly pilfered by the guards, and prisoners considered themselves lucky if they got half of what their families managed to collect for them at great hardship and toil in a land where virtually everything needed by human beings is in short supply.

Criminal Guards

The guards on the Isle of Pines, as elsewhere in Cuba, are simply the former common criminals. The overwhelming majority of these offenders are Negroes. In fact, when he ordered their freedom, Fidel Castro spoke of the injustice of imprisoning a poor Negro, who might have merely stolen a chicken because he was hungry. Actually most of these common criminals were long-term, case-hardened offenders— murderers, rapists, sadists, perverts. In addition to being naturally cruel, many, if not most, of them had a strong racial resentment toward the whites, who had formerly ruled as their superiors. When their latent hatred was not strong enough, the Communists would fan it with lying propaganda. This is a calculated stage in Castro's race war. It has no rational limits. The alternatives he is presenting to the white officials, managers, professionals and intellectuals are either total subordination to the Communist movement or slow extermination.

In addition to psychological torture, prisoners who commit the slightest infraction of the rules are placed in special punishment cells. These pigsties are scarcely large enough for one man, but seven to nine prisoners are crowded in each of them. Men are put in the punishment cells completely naked. They are doused with cold water and the floor of these cells is almost always covered with water. The prisoners must move their bowels in an open hole in full view of the rest. The only water for bathing and washing one's plate is a thin trickle over the open latrine.

Following the Playa Girón [Bay of Pigs] invasion of April 17, 1962, Castro ordered every *circular* mined with 2,000 pounds of dynamite or plastic explosives. The guards told the prisoners that, in the event of another anti-Castro armed movement, the first act of the government would be to blow up the prison.

Castro has always feared an American attack on the Isle of Pines and for that reason has turned the Island into a fortress. Before the Russians took over in late 1962, there were about 16,000 militiamen stationed there. The Island was seeded with gun emplacements and protected by tanks and Migs [Soviet fighter jets].

Violence Toward Prisoners

The *requisas* [prisonwide searches] in the Isle of Pines prison are incredibly brutal. The *circulares* are first surrounded by tanks, assault cars, machine guns and ordinary troops. At a signal, the military open fire on the apertures of the *circulares* that face outward. This always causes a large number of wounds and, because of the *requisas*, there are prisoners who have lost eyes, legs and arms. When this preliminary fire is over, the prisoners are sometimes forced out of the *circulares* at bayonet point, which causes more wounds and even death.

When the prisoners are outside, the black guards proceed with their search and, in the process, steal anything that is of value to them.

Standard operating procedure in a *requisa* is to force the men to stand closely packed together in lines and more or less at attention. This is required during the whole period of the search, which may last twenty-four hours or more. Men fall out of line and faint. Sometimes, their comrades are allowed to pick them up; at other times, they simply lie there in the dirt. A guard may tell a prisoner to stick his tongue out, to look up at the sky or to turn his head and, if he doesn't move fast enough, the guard will club him with the butt end of his rifle.

During the whole procedure, there is no food or water for the prisoners. The men stand in burning sun or heavy rain unprotected. Regardless of weather, the *requisa* goes on.

There have been two hunger strikes on the Isle of Pines. The first was caused by hunger. The politicals stayed on hunger strike for seven days in protest against the fact that they were served only one meal, consisting of a plate of macaroni or a broth. The second strike was in protest against the fact that two prisoners, who were planning to escape, were viciously beaten and tortured. Despite the fact that both strikes were lost, the morale and solidarity of the political prisoners is reported unbroken at the time these lines are written—that is to say, in May of 1963.

One of the hunger strikes was smashed by bringing up tanks, which blew open the doors of the *circulares* with the fire of their heavy guns. The prisoners were forced out of the cells at bayonet point. Those who were slow or resisted orders were viciously stabbed. In this *requisa*, seven men were bayoneted to death. Among those bayoneted was David Salvador, the first head of the Confederation of Cuban Labor (CTC) under Fidel Castro and a man who was my fellow prisoner in La Cabaña.

Some 250 men were wounded in this search. There was no alcohol in the infirmary, no bandages, nothing with which to suture wounds, no sulpha or antibiotics. The victims were left untended. The wounds festered. I was told that about 10 per cent of the prisoners on the Island had tuberculosis and that fungus conditions were rampant.

The director of this prison is a Guatemalan Communist and a confidential agent of Jacobo Arbenz, the former Red President of that country. This man, who is called Tarrau, is a lieutenant in the Castro Army. He does not dare to appear in the *circulares* without his guard of from thirty to forty heavily armed men. Tarrau had the prisoners who plotted an escape beaten and tortured before his eyes and in the presence of the others.

Exceptions to the Rule

Not all of the Cuban political prisoners on the Island suffer under these abominable conditions. There are exceptions. When I returned to the United States, I learned from Cuban exiles that one of them was Major Huber Matos, the hero of the Cuban Revolution who broke with Castro on the issue of Communist domination and was sentenced to a long term on the Isle of Pines.

I was informed that Huber Matos enjoys unprecedented privileges, that he has a room of his own, eats special food, has unique visiting privileges and is allowed to go about in the uniform of an officer of Castro's Rebel Army.

Another enjoying the same special privileges was Davíd Salvador, the anti-American labor agitator who was so active in the Castro blood purge. He even has his own television set.

This is in sharp contrast with the sanguinary vengeance Castro inflicts on those of his close associates who broke with him decisively and completely.

Many Cubans suspect that Matos is being held in reserve in case Castro decides to "liberalize" his dictatorship by including some "anti-Communists" in the Cabinet as a means of getting U.S. support. Certainly, Matos is being built up by leftwing American writers, such as the former Communist, Theodore Draper, as a hope for anti-communism in Cuba.

The condition of the Bay of Pigs invaders in the Isle of Pines prison was better than that of the rest of the politicals. Since there was a chance of selling them for ransom, they were kept in reasonably good physical shape. By contrast, James D. Beane of Franklinville, North Carolina, charged with counterrevolution, is lame and unable to stand on his feet. My friend, Robert Geddes Morton, the former head of the Pepsi-Cola Company in Cuba, was suffering from severe tuberculosis when he was sent to the Isle of Pines. He was finally released in February, 1963. I was shocked to learn that this man I had believed to be in his fifties, was actually only 31!

The 5,000 or so Cubans and Americans, imprisoned on

the Isle of Pines, are being slowly murdered under conditions of unspeakable brutality and slow torture. The liberation of these prisoners and of other fighters for Cuban freedom, held elsewhere on the island, is a duty for all of us who believe in justice and liberty. Their emancipation, however, should be the result of the application of force—economic, political or military—against the Castro dictatorship and not the result of payment of ransom.

The Women's Prisons

There are two women's prisons: Guanajay in the province of Havana and Baracoa in Oriente province. The female guards are the former inmates—common criminals and all of them colored. Many of these women guards are notorious for being hardened Lesbians.

The women prisoners are forced to wear dungarees, shirts and boots and are not allowed to wear any female adornment at all. There are farms attached to the prisons where the politicals are worked like beasts of burden. Guanajay has close to 2,000 women prisoners and Baracoa about 5,000.

In July 1962, at the same time as on the Isle of Pines, there was a hunger strike on Guanajay. News of this came through relatives of the women prisoners who had passed the word along to our visitors and other sources of information. *The strike was in protest against a requisa which had lasted two days.*

The Prison System

According to Communists in La Cabaña, who discussed the situation with me, there were from 75,000 to 150,000 political prisoners in Cuba in the fall of 1962. This amounted to from 1 to 3 per cent of the entire population.

The Cuban prison system is closely modelled on Soviet practice. The stages of imprisonment are characterized by progressively increasing severity. Thus, when a person is arrested, he is generally first taken to the city hall, where his family can visit him and bring him food. From this place of temporary detention, he may be sent to the G-2 headquarters, which should under no circumstances be confused with the G-2 torture farms. Here things are considerably tougher, but the prisoner can still have visits twice a week from female members of his family and can still receive food from the outside. The third stage may be La Cabaña or El Principe, both of which are considerably worse than the G-2 headquarters. Once in La Cabaña, the prisoner generally faces two alternatives: execution or shipment to the Isle of Pines.

The Communist rehabilitation program . . . is patterned on the same theory of progressive change, except that here the direction is reversed and, with each advance in indoctrination and obedience, there is a further step in improvement of material conditions and freedom.

The same strategy was applied toward visitors. On the first occasion, they would be treated with consideration. The second time, especially if the prisoner—husband or son—had been recalcitrant toward authority, the visitors would be treated with roughness or brutality. The women would be stripped naked and searched by Lesbian guards, who would pinch and feel them. They would be made to jump in the air naked with their legs spread apart so that anything they had concealed could be detected. This was done to children visitors also. The problem did not arise in the case of men visitors, for, as a rule, none are allowed in Cuban prisons.

When the prisoner reaches his final stage of degradation, the Isle of Pines, every obstacle is placed in the way of would-be visitors; they are subjected to every possible inconvenience and molestation; they are treated like enemies of the state, and, at best, they are able to see their men three or four times in a year.

Chapter 2

Building and Defending Socialism

Chapter Preface

In a sense, the Cuban Revolution did not begin until after the ousting of Fulgencio Batista in 1959. Fulfilling the promises of the rebels meant completely reordering the Cuban economy, and with it, the society. Over the next forty-plus years, the revolution's two greatest challenges were modernizing the economy and coping with U.S. hostility.

Like most Socialist nations, Cuba at first tried to industrialize rapidly. But it soon became clear that Cuba was much better suited to focus on agriculture rather than manufacturing as a means of enriching the lives of the Cuban people. From the mid-1960s on, Castro's regime worked diligently to apply modern scientific and technological advances to the production of cash crops such as sugar and tobacco that could be sold throughout the world at lucrative prices.

Unfortunately, the United States presented a major roadblock to these plans. Once Cuba's largest trading partner, it refused to trade with Cuba after it became clear that Castro was a Socialist and an ally of the Soviet Union, America's Cold War nemesis. Cuba managed to find eager trading partners in other parts of the world, especially the Communist nations of Europe and Asia, but it was never able to replace the trade lost as a result of the U.S. embargo.

In addition to working to undermine Cuban foreign trade, the United States also worked to overthrow the Castro regime by force. In 1961 it backed an invasion of Cuban expatriates at Playa Girón, or the Bay of Pigs. The invasion failed miserably and served only to embarrass the United States and enhance Castro's popularity at home. However, the abortive invasion led in part to the creation of a garrison state in Cuba, the result of which was the diversion of badly needed resources to equip and maintain a large standing army.

Planning the Economy by Involving the People

Che Guevara

When Castro took control of Cuba, one of his first steps was to revitalize the Cuban economy. Under Fulgencio Batista, the economy had stagnated under the control of U.S. and European capitalists, and it produced very little that was of value to the average Cuban. Castro set out to rectify this situation by building factories to produce the basic industrial products, such as cement and ammonia, that were needed to industrialize the economy. He also set out to educate the Cuban people so they could serve as technicians in Cuba's new industrial establishments. After several years of attempting to impose socialism on the economy, in 1962 Cuba's first economic plan went into effect.

Ernesto "Che" Guevara was an Argentine doctor and one of Castro's earliest recruits. He fought in Cuba as a guerrilla and eventually became one of Castro's top advisers. In this excerpt from a televised speech in 1961, when he was the minister of industries, Guevara outlines the steps by which the Cuban government was developing its first nationwide economic plan. The speech emphasizes his belief that any such plan must be developed by consulting with the workers who will be entrusted with making it work.

Che Guevara, *Che Guevara Speaks: Selected Speeches and Writings*, edited by George Lavan. New York: Pathfinder Press, 1967.

The process of state acquisition of the means of production is following two more or less parallel roads: one is the logical and conscious course toward defined goals by a state whose decrees and laws have nationalized the principal industries; the other is the result of the collective fears of a defeated class and the political commotions that have continued uninterruptedly over these last two years.

There is a series of laws, including some laws administered by the Ministry of Public Works through the office of its Under Secretary for the Recovery of Property, which at first confiscated corruptly acquired property—an indiscriminate assortment, both large and small—and at present confiscates the property of individuals committing acts against the security of the state.

So that when the great split occurred in the petty bourgeoisie, one part—the most conscious, most ideologically wide awake, most patriotic, most courageous, possessing not even small means of production—took the side of the state, of the revolution, of the people, and began to take up their tasks and integrate themselves into the revolution. The other part, however, remaining subservient—especially ideologically, and frequently economically—to the bourgeoisie, which was in the process of being defeated, began to plot or to flee directly abroad. And through this process it left a string of small enterprises that the Ministry had to take over in order to provide work for the employees.

This has been a continuous process. Unfortunately, although we have tried to stem it by offering guarantees, the temptation held out by the North American power has proved greater than our pledges, and small industrialists and merchants—sometimes tempted by the idea of returning as conquerors, other times simply out of fear, other times with the idea in mind of winning a little gold braid at home in the mountains somewhere or in underground work—have engaged in conspiratorial actions and been discovered by our immense intelligence service, the entire Cuban people.

As a result then, we get the gift, by no means a welcome one, of a shed with seven workers, without sanitary facilities, without the slightest mechanization, without the most elementary notion of organization. But there are seven men who have to have work because they have to feed their families. Naturally, we take them in as best we can and try to rationalize the industry in time. . . .

Developing an Economic Plan

The first precondition is control over the means of production. The *sine qua non* [essential element] for an economic plan is that the state control the bulk of the means of production, and better yet, if possible, all the means of production.

That is, what this shows is that a real economic plan is a centralized state plan based on a socialist conception of the economy. But all this may be, and in our case it was, just the first step. We have control of the means of production. Can you make a plan with control of the means of production alone? It cannot be done. To make a plan you have to have a clear picture of the national reality. That is, you must have firm, precise, detailed statistical knowledge of all economic factors; and that is a problem. Because we in Cuba all know, and all our foreign visitors know, that the basic characteristic of economic colonialism, as it is of capitalism, is anarchy, the absence of sound statistical data which would give us a clear picture of the situation.

The government is hard at work to complete this phase, and the statistical data-gathering phase is virtually completed. Once we have the statistical knowledge and control over the means of production, we must make certain of our goals. You have to have a clear idea of your goals, where you want to go, by what means and how fast you want to reach these goals. And once you are clear about that, you have to have a proper balance sheet. Because there is a certain reality. You can say, to put it in practical terms, to make it easier to understand: We are going to build so many schools that in five years' time we won't need one more school in Cuba; we are going to build so many houses that in five years' time we won't need one more house in Cuba; we are going to build a merchant fleet of the sort that in five years' time we won't need one more boat in Cuba; we are going to build so many airplanes that in five years' time not a single foreign airplane will be needed in Cuba.

We can keep on making plans like that, but when we come to drawing up a balance sheet—that is, to comparing all we want with what we can do—we see that this cannot be done. Because it is not materially possible to satisfy in five years' time all the needs of people who have hungered for centuries for even a crust of bread.

Then comes the stage of sitting down and balancing the plan, taking out here, taking out there, trying to make sure that the plan gives the necessary emphasis to the points I indicated, . . . creation of enterprises which in turn create new means of production. But we must not neglect the other points, that is, the creation of means of production properly speaking, buying means of production abroad, even if it means holding the speed of the country's industrial development back a bit.

When you have all these things, it still doesn't add up to a plan. You need at least two other most important ingredients. One is a guiding body. That is, in capitalist anarchy, a plan is impossible. Where the capitalists fight for a market and sacrifice everything to obtain this market, an internal market, there can be no plan. A plan must without fail have unity of direction and unity and firmness of leadership. In this country, this unity is provided by the Central Planning Board whose chairman is the premier himself and whose vice-chairman, I might add, is our deputy premier, Comandante Raúl Castro. The highest political authorities in this country directly manage the plan, guide it and give it the unity of command necessary for its fulfillment.

I remind you that we are still engaged in the plan's preliminary tasks. The plan commences in 1962. We are gathering data, getting a clear idea of what we want and how we can get it in the framework of our balance.

There is still one final point without which an economic development plan is impossible in a socialist system, and that is understanding and support of the plan by the people. A plan is not a mechanical thing, the product of semi-metaphysical, cold scientific labors in some office and then transmitted downward. A plan is a living thing whose fundamental purpose is to find the country's idle reserves and put them to work in production. To do that you must galvanize the great factor of production—the people. The people must understand what we want, discuss our aims in each instance, present their counterviews; and once they have understood it and approved it, the plan can go forward. That is, the natural course is from the top down, but from there it returns to the top.

In other words, the leaders of a country in close identification with their people consider what is best for the people and put that into numbers, more or less arbitrary though, of course, based on logic and judgment, and send them from the top down: for example, from the Central Planning Board to the Ministry of Industries, where the Ministry of Industries makes the corrections it deems appropriate since it is closer to certain aspects of real life than the other offices. From there it continues downward to the enterprises, which make other corrections. From the enterprises it goes to the factories, where other corrections are made, and from there to the workers who must have the final say on the plan.

That is, a plan is profoundly democratic in its execution and that is its essential basis. In considering what is wanted in a development plan, no one in this country, or any country where there is social justice, proposes development for the sake of better personal incomes or personal successes. Development is to better the country so that each person will individually obtain a better income and a better life. If this is the case, everyone in the country has and must have an interest in the plan. Therefore, it must be thoroughly understood, reach the masses, be discussed and not mechanically approved but studied. . . .

Training a New Kind of Technician

We are trying to create something entirely new. That is, a man who comes from the working class, from the peasantry, who is a product of the revolution—those children who came out of the Sierra Maestra, not knowing what an electric light was, who are becoming trained agronomists in schools like the Camilo Cienfuegos School, will be the base for the new technicians of the future. They will feel totally at one with the people. They will not have the least feeling of inferiority or superiority toward anyone.

Our technicians have had their faults, but despite everything, despite the fact that technicians of the old type are not the ideal, we would have preferred them to none. And in many cases we have had to resign ourselves to none; because either there weren't any—in general there were far fewer than needed—or they left and each day there are some leaving. It is no secret to anybody that each day somebody—because he has been bought or, to be fair, because he simply can't stand the "climate" in Cuba, an entirely new climate—takes the road of exile. I don't think it is as smooth a road as many imagine, but that is the reality.

So we have had a whole series of problems. That is, a lack of technical knowledge and a low ideological consciousness on the part of technicians, of whom, moreover, we haven't had so many. Thus construction has been hard and continues hard. We have had to resort to training or to semi-training en masse of *compañeros* with a poor educational background. We have had to teach the people how to read and write and, after they have learned that, to give them responsibilities requiring considerable knowledge—at the very least reading, writing, and the techniques involved in their jobs; but everything must be created in this way. That is the great work of construction. That is the miracle a people can accomplish when they are filled with the holy idea of production, with an entirely revitalized spirit, when they are in the really dangerous position of creating a new world under unfavorable conditions and at great speed—which is our situation. . . .

Hearing the Voices of Workers

We have already talked about almost all the problems of industrialization. Now I want to emphasize relations with the workers.

We have already seen what urgent need there is for relations with the masses. But, of course, this is not a fault, let us say, on our side alone. It is a fault on both sides. . . .

For example, we have a creation of the revolution—a few days ago I was reading a little news sheet we have here. . . . It said that the Technical Advisory Committees were created by the timorous petty bourgeoisie in the government in order to give the masses, who were demanding the right to run the factories, something—without in reality giving them anything.

Now from the theoretical standpoint, that is an absurdity and from the practical standpoint it is infamous, or else grossly mistaken. The trouble in fact with the Technical Advisory Committees is that they were not created by mass pressure: They were bureaucratically created from the top to give the masses a vehicle they had not asked for, and that is the fault of the masses. We, the "timorous petty bourgeoisie," went looking for a channel that would enable us to listen to the masses' voice. That is what I want to emphasize. And we created the Technical Advisory Committees, for better or worse, with the imperfections they very likely have, because they were our idea, our creation, that is, the creation of people who lack experience in these problems. What was not present at all, and I want to stress that, was mass pressure. And there must be mass pressure in a whole series of things, because the masses must take an interest in finding out what a plan is, what industrialization is, what each factory must do, what their duty is, and how this duty can be added to or reduced, what the workers' interests are in every factory. All these are problems that must stir the masses.

The masses must be constantly abreast of what is happening in their work centers and be able to relate it to the overall life of the nation.

We intend to continue discussions in order to increase the effectiveness of the Technical Advisory Committees, whose importance has been added to by the fact that they are now at work in the Replacement Parts Committees, also created from above by the revolution. We want to establish ties—not ties because ties are very narrow—instruments for expression that will enable the mass to make itself heard automatically at the top. Because it is a sure thing that somebody up in a ministry, closed in, with air conditioning and all those things, cannot hear the pulse of the workers, and that is why we are looking for instruments for expression.

We are trying in every way possible to improve this situation, to make the workers feel a deep involvement in their revolution. And for this we have two very important plans—one will be announced right about now, will be presented to the public: the national emulation plan.

Emulation Plan

What do they consist of?—I can get ahead of things—the national emulation plan is divided into two phases. Its second phase will be, let us say, a technical plan that will have work quotas, and these quotas will have rewards along with them. In all, there will be a perfect adjustment of production, productivity, and reward. This reward is fundamentally a moral stimulus, as well as having its material side.

The first phase of the emulation plan, which is the important one, is the organizational phase. What must be the objects of workers' emulation? They must keep their factories clean, their machines in perfect condition, give thought to replacement parts and see how they can be made, see that raw materials are secured, replace raw materials when not imported, guard their work centers, not only their machines but their work centers, as collective organs of production, from any attempts at sabotage, join revolutionary organizations which defend the revolution, raise their technical level, raise their technical level above all else, contribute by their work, their brains and their study to the country's production.

All this will be laid out in a plan, as I say, in two stages. The first stage is, let us say, the organization of the emulation plan. The second is emulation, properly speaking, or in its scientifically worked out form.

The education plan includes from the lowest levels—we are not going to divide this up into levels, that is also a bad

habit, petty bourgeois, as the Trotskyist *compañeros* say—
from the lowest to the highest technical capabilities.

For example, we are starting with the minimum technical
capability. What is the minimum technical capability? The
minimum is what is needed by an individual to operate the
machines on his job. Then a series of primary schools will
be established; afterwards, institutes, universities which will
bring the workers along in a continuous chain, from the il-
literate workers who reach minimum technical competence
to highly qualified engineers, to the president of the republic or whatever, through a continuous chain in which work
and study combined carry forward the technical training of
the workers and educate them in every way.

That is the great task not only of the Ministry of Industries; the Ministry of Industries has, let us say, the initial part
in the plan. That is, it must seek the worker of inquiring
mind, give him his first instruction, establish schools of elementary administration. After this it is the turn of the Ministry of Education, the Council of Ministers, or the Central
Planning Board for special kinds of advanced study.

Moving Forward with Socialism

All this looks fine on paper; like everything else, many of
these things don't turn out in practice as well as they are described on paper. But what is fundamental in all this is that
this work would be impossible without two things: One is
the country's own determination to do it; the other is the
help of the socialist countries. Both are completely bound
together and complementary, since the socialist countries
offer their aid because they see our country is eager to improve, to liberate itself. And when our country feels that it
has support, it feels more secure, shows greater firmness, a
greater urge to accomplish things; and more help comes
from the socialist countries. But these are two highly inter-
connected things.

A very rapid struggle of blows and counterblows brought
the Cuban people from the revolution of high ideals—which
for just a few months, yet some months, was no danger to

imperialism—to our present profound socialist revolution, which owns the means of production and plans the economy *in toto* [in total]. . . .

As far as we are concerned, in our duty, in our work in the Ministry of Industries, we have to know that what characterizes socialism is that the people own the means of production and that these are put to their service. Naturally, we will have to talk a lot about the new historical stage through which we are living; we will have to explain very clearly that, besides the purely economic side, there is a side having to do with consciousness, which is of the utmost importance. . . .

It is important to stress that unless the people are clearly conscious of their rights and duties in this new stage, we cannot truly attain, cannot really work in the kind of socialist society to which we aspire—a socialist society which is absolutely democratic, which is democratic by definition, because it bases itself on the needs, on the aspirations, of the people, a socialist society where the people play a determining role.

Repelling the
Imperialist Invaders

Orlando Castro Hidalgo

Fidel Castro's victory over the forces of Fulgencio Batista in
1959 put him in command of the Cuban government. In 1961
his command was challenged by an invasion of U.S.-backed
Cuban expatriates. The invaders landed at two beaches on the
Bay of Pigs, on the opposite end of the island from Havana,
hoping that the invasion would incite a popular uprising
against Castro. Instead, the Cuban people remained loyal to
Castro while the Cuban military drove the invaders off the
island after three days of hard fighting. The victory solidified
Castro's control because it secured the confidence and support of the Cuban people, who now regarded Castro as the
savior of their nation. This support allowed him to continue to
build socialism on the island for the next forty-plus years.

Orlando Castro Hidalgo fought as a pro-Castro guerrilla
during the revolution. After the revolution he became a
policeman in Havana. He eventually was promoted to the
diplomatic corps and trained as a spy. In 1961 he was serving
in a police combat battalion that had been specially trained to
defend beaches against amphibious landings. In this excerpt,
he describes how his unit fought against the U.S.-backed
Cuban invaders at Playa Girón, better known in the United
States as the Bay of Pigs.

A great deal has been said and written about the ill-fated
Bay of Pigs invasion of April 1961. The planning and

preparation, the last-minute crippling of the attack by the cancellation of further air raids on airfields, the lack of sufficient logistical support and air cover over the beachhead—all these are now history. The politicians have told their stories, the invaders have told theirs, but not much has ever been said by the foot sloggers on the government side who fought the invaders toe to toe. I was one of those infantrymen.

Early in 1961 it was public knowledge that Cuban exiles were building a military force in Central America. Whether these would be infiltrated into Cuba to carry out guerrilla operations, or whether a full-blown invasion was planned, was not clear. Cuba prepared for an attack. Completing its work in the Escambray Mountains, the police company to which I was attached was moved to Ganuza Beach in Matanzas Province to await a possible invasion. After several weeks, the unit was again transferred, this time to a camp known as El Esperón, near Caimito de Guayabal in Pinar del Río Province.

The Invasion Begins

Early in the morning of April 15 air raids were carried out on several Cuban airfields. At El Esperón the *alarma de combate* was given, and we were told that the raids undoubtedly were the prelude to an invasion. The following day warships were seen off the coast of Pinar del Río (actually, this was a feint by the U.S. Navy to distract attention from the main landing point on the south coast of Matanzas).

On the morning of April 17, Monday, the camp loudspeakers sounded reveille at Esperón and we were quickly summoned into formation. We were told that enemy forces had carried out landings, and we must be prepared for battle. All leaves had been canceled following the Saturday air raids, and this cancellation remained in effect. Rumors flashed through the camp: a tremendous attack was coming, the Americans were going to land, heavy air raids were in prospect.

That afternoon the entire Police Combat Battalion was ordered to march to the nearby coast. (The battalion consisted of five companies of about ninety men each. I belonged to the Fifth Platoon of the Fourth Company. I led a seven-man squad.) We were set to work digging trenches. Five feet deep and zigzag in design, the trenches extended (although not continuously) for dozens of miles along the coast and the base of hills close by. Army and militia units also participated in the task. The trench-digging continued through most of the night, but the enemy did not appear.

When the digging was completed, we camouflaged the trenches with leaves and branches. We slept in the trenches as best we could—a sleep occasionally interrupted by false combat alarms sounded by sergeants who wanted to test their men.

At noon of April 18 we were called into formation and were informed we would be transported to the theater of operations, where the enemy had landed. Late that afternoon huge trucks arrived at the camp, and we climbed aboard. The ride lasted about four hours. We knew the general area in which we were heading, although not the precise point. We wondered and worried about what lay ahead for us, and thought of our families and sweethearts. Some took photographs of loved ones from their wallets and stared at them. Regrets were voiced, and there were complaints and occasional jokes, and some singing, too.

I was in an open truck and was able to recognize areas I knew, as we drove through. Then, as we approached the south coast, we began passing ambulances and small trucks converted to ambulances. From our trucks we could see that these vehicles were carrying wounded militiamen and soldiers of the regular Army, but we saw no one in any other uniform, no members of the invading force. This impressed us; we realized the significance of what we saw: the invaders must indeed be fighting hard in order to be causing these casualties.

Going into Combat

The trucks slowed to a stop by the road, and we jumped out. Sporadic firing could be heard in the distance. An airplane

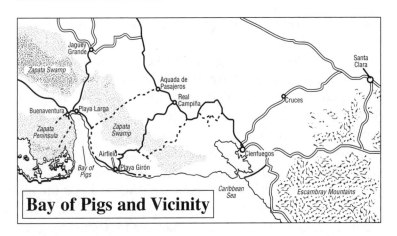

Bay of Pigs and Vicinity

was heard overhead, and antiaircraft guns opened fire. The tracer bullets streaming through the dark sky were our first sight of combat.

We were warned to be on the alert for mines reportedly placed in the ground. The men gathered to get into formation, and as I stepped through sand, I felt a solid object under one of my booted feet. The foot suddenly developed a mind of its own; it refused to move further. I leaned over slowly and began to brush the sand away from my foot. Men near me noticed what was happening, and they stiffened, staring. My fingers felt hard, smooth matter. My heart beat rapidly, and I was close to panic. I gingerly continued brushing away the sand, and to my vast relief I was able to discern that what I was stepping on was only a large conch shell. The breath I exhaled was equaled by those of the men standing nearby.

The place at which we had arrived was near Larga Beach, although we could not see the ocean from where we were. This was a sandy area, spotted with rocks, clumps of shrubs, and mangrove trees. Burnt shrubbery and overturned buses gave evidence of recent combat. The buses had been transporting militia from the city of Cienfuegos and had been spotted and attacked by the invaders' aircraft.

We were told to make ourselves as comfortable as possible while awaiting further orders. We sprawled along the side of the road, our eyes warily searching the ground for signs of mines. Several men used their knapsacks as makeshift pillows.

We wore olive-green fatigues and kepis of the same color. We were equipped with Belgian rifles and Czech submachine guns, more than 200 rounds of ammunition each, and Soviet-made shovels and pickaxes. These were found to break easily, and most were discarded.

We remained in the area the rest of the night and until seven-thirty in the morning. Reports that were received indicated that there had been heavy fighting and that the invaders were in possession of some territory. We heard that the main damage to the invaders had been inflicted by government planes attacking the landing ships. We got little sleep that night. We listened to occasional firing in the distance, and talked among ourselves, knowing we would soon be in combat.

In the morning we were told we would march toward the enemy positions at Girón. Two lines were formed, on either side of the road, with about six feet between each man. We watched the skies: earlier a B-26 had skimmed in low, firing its machine guns, but had been driven off by antiaircraft fire. I had thought bullets were striking near me, but found that these were only the expended shells of the AA guns.

In titular command of the police battalion was the chief of police, Major Efigenio Ameijeiras, who arrived that morning. In actual command was Major Samuel Rodiles, a veteran of the 1956–1958 guerrilla war. Ameijeiras said he would lead his men into combat. Later, however, when contact with the enemy was established and firing began, he was seen heading toward the rear. We heard that he had been summoned by Fidel Castro.

A Slow Advance

The precise location of the invaders was unknown, and we therefore did not know just when we would go into battle. At nine o'clock in the morning we scrambled off the road when a B-26 came in on a strafing run. Two men in my company were hit.

That morning, before we had set out on our march, an Army officer had warned Ameijeiras not to try to advance. The officer reported that the invaders were fighting well, that probably they were made up of veterans of Korea and World War II, and that they had inflicted heavy casualties on the government forces, suffering few themselves. Whenever the government troops attempted to advance, he said, they were thrown back. Despite this news and advice, Ameijeiras declared that we would move forward, even if this were to be a suicidal advance.

As we marched ahead, it appeared that we might very well be involved in a suicidal attack. We passed militiamen seated by the side of the road, who, although they did not seem to be retreating, were not moving forward either. We noted considerable numbers of casualties not yet picked up by the ambulances. Questioned as to what the general situation was, the militia replied: "Every time we have gone into battle we have been repulsed. Many of our men have been killed." Asked to join our advance, the militia answered that they were awaiting their superiors, but these were nowhere to be seen.

We found one militia leader, but he refused to advance. He was promptly relieved of his command. The second-in-command of our police battalion, Captain Ricardo Carbó, took charge of the militia unit and got the men to move forward with us.

The road led over the beach, the ocean to the right of the men and swampland to their left. At around ten in the morning we received the first indications that we were entering combat: mortar shells fell into the ocean offshore, sending up great geysers of spray. Someone said that this was the Army carrying out target practice, and with this explanation we continued marching ahead. (Actually, these were shells from the invaders. Captured later on, their mortar men mentioned that they had been disconcerted when, upon dropping their shells near the advancing lines, they had seen the police unconcernedly continue to move forward.)

We came under enemy infantry fire, and our advance was

now slow and exceedingly dangerous. I moved forward as best I could, at times running in a low crouch, sometimes slithering ahead on my stomach, going from shelter to shelter, a rock here, a hole in the sand there. The enemy mortar fire improved its aim, and the police casualties mounted. A member of my squad stood up to run forward, and at that precise moment was killed by the nearby explosion of a mortar shell. And then another man in the squad was killed. The company as a whole suffered some ten dead and a considerable number of wounded.

The invaders were fighting well. Nevertheless, we were able to advance. We pushed beyond Larga Beach, the enemy pulling back slowly, while maintaining heavy fire on the government forces.

Tanks to the Rescue?

At one point around noon, we were pinned down by concentrated fire from enemy machine gun nests. The advance appeared to be halted. It was then that six Soviet-built tanks arrived on the scene, much to our relief. The tanks blasted their way through the enemy strong points, forcing the invaders back again. We charged, following the tanks. The fast-moving tanks pulled ahead of us.

Soon after, however, we saw tanks coming back down the road. At first we thought these were enemy vehicles, but then recognized them as the same tanks that had been leading the advance. One of our officers waved down a tank and demanded to know why the tanks were pulling back. A soldier in the tank replied that they were having difficulty with their oil. The officer angrily asked: "How come it works to retreat? Why doesn't it work to advance?"

The tank men ignored the officer's remonstrations, saying they did not have to account to him. They closed the tank hatch. The infuriated officer tried to put his rifle into a slit in the tank with the evident intention of shooting its crew. Other men seized the officer and took away his weapon.

The tank rapidly proceeded back to the rear, as did three

others. Their haste was so great that they ran over and killed a wounded man lying in their path. Other soldiers had to jump out of their way in order to avoid being crushed.

The tanks were retreating because two of their number had been destroyed by an enemy Sherman tank emplaced at a curve in the road. The Soviet-made tanks were especially vulnerable due to the fact that they carried, attached to their sides, fuel tanks which burst into flames when hit by gunfire.

There had been other instances of cowardice during the advance. At one point, an order was passed through the ranks to a certain unit telling it to move to the vanguard position. When the order reached that unit, most of the men denied belonging to it. On another occasion, a police captain hiding in a hole ordered his men to move forward, but refrained from doing so himself. A sergeant came over and wrathfully berated the officer, and followed this by socking him in the face.

The enemy tank that had forced the government tank column to retreat had situated itself among dense vegetation in a ravine, protected by rocks. The curve near which the tank was emplaced became known as the "Death Curve" because of the heavy fighting at this spot. A bazooka unit circled through the swamps on the left with the intention of striking the tank, but ran into enemy machine gun nests and had to pull back. Upon returning to the government lines, the unit's members were mistaken for enemy troops, and we opened fire on them. After a great deal of frantic yelling, the men managed to identify themselves and the firing ceased.

The Sherman was finally put out of action when a lieutenant fired a bazooka shot which scored a direct hit on it. The advance was able to continue, and we approached the town of Girón itself. (It is by the name of this town, rather than by the Bay of Pigs, that the invasion is officially known in Cuba.)

At three in the afternoon a heavy mortar attack rained down on us. There was another damaged and abandoned Sherman tank to one side of the road, and I headed toward it to find shelter from the close and continuous hail of shells.

Wounded

A loud explosion close by—I felt and heard it, but saw nothing. I was being wafted through the air. There was no pain—I did not really know what was happening to me—perhaps I was dying . . . then after a second or two I lost consciousness.

I awoke slowly. My memory returned and I recalled the explosion. I was lying on a floor somewhere. It seemed to be nighttime, and I wondered whether I was a prisoner. My head throbbed with pain; it felt as if the whole thing were inflamed. I found that there was blood in my nose and mouth, and that I had received no medical treatment. I touched the blood, tasted it, thought bleakly, "I've been destroyed." I was terrified that I had lost my sight. I realized there were other human beings about, and I touched one nearby and felt cold flesh. The man was probably dead.

I learned later that my eyesight had been temporarily impaired and that I had received a wound on my forehead.

I heard a voice that I recognized. It was that of Juan de Dios, a member of my company who had been wounded earlier. I called out to him, startling him, because he thought all those around him were dead. De Dios came over and told me that we were in an improvised hospital in Jagüey Grande. He was able to get two attendants to place me on a stretcher and bandage me. Then I was taken to a hospital in another city. Here I was X-rayed and given necessary treatment. After a week, I was transferred to the Police Hospital in Havana, where I remained an additional three weeks.

In the meantime, the invasion had been repelled and destroyed, and Fidel Castro was in firm control of Cuba.

Relying on Agriculture to Boost the Economy

Fidel Castro with Lee Lockwood

Like Russia after the success of the Bolshevik Revolution, Cuba under Castro worked diligently to build up its industrial base. Within a few years, however, Castro realized that Cuba's future did not lie with rapid industrialization (which under Joseph Stalin in the USSR had wreaked societal havoc among the Soviet people). Rather, the island's climate and soil, coupled with a growing world demand for food and a growing world glut of manufactured goods, dictated that Cuba should develop economically by applying modern science and technology to agriculture.

Lee Lockwood was an American photojournalist who first met Castro in 1959, just a few days after Fulgencio Batista had fled Cuba. Over the next six years, Lockwood made three more extended visits to Cuba, each time conversing at length with Castro. In this excerpt, taken from a seven-day conversation between Lockwood and Castro on the Isle of Pines, Castro explains why Cuba has shifted the focus of its economic development from industry to agriculture.

L OCKWOOD: But is agriculture really so important that you yourself must spend all this time on it?

CASTRO: What does agricultural development mean to our country? It means the quickest satisfaction of the fundamental needs of the people: food, clothing, and shelter. It means the immediate utilization of the major natural resources which our country possesses. What are they? The resources of our soil and of our climate. Our being situated in a semitropical zone offers us exceptional conditions for cultivating certain crops. For example, there is no other country in the world, in my opinion, that has the natural conditions for the production of sugar cane that Cuba has.

We also possess exceptional conditions for livestock production. We are able to make use of pastures all year round, and I think our per-acre productivity of meat and milk can be double that of any industrialized country of Europe; likewise tropical fruits, which are becoming more and more in demand in the world. Here on the Isle of Pines alone we are going to have an area planted with citrus trees as extensive as all of that which Israel has, and we expect to achieve a yield as high as theirs per acre. It is possible that Cuba's overall national production of citrus fruits will come to triple theirs between 1970 and 1975, when the groves will come into full production. That will make us the leading exporters in the world. We also have good conditions for growing winter vegetables, fibers, and precious woods, including some types that are found only on our soil.

With these natural resources and with a relatively small investment in farm machinery, seeds, fertilizers, and insecticides, and with the labor of the people, we will be able in a very short time to recover our investments and at the same time to obtain a considerable surplus for exportation.

The Pre-Revolution Economy

Of course, the possibilities of which I am speaking also existed before the Revolution. That is, the natural conditions were the same. What was lacking? Markets. We lacked both internal and external markets. The internal market was limited by the quantity of men and women working in the country and by the salaries which they earned. The external market was limited by a policy of compromise, which prevented Cuba from taking advantage of all the existing possibilities for world trade.

Almost all our trade was with the United States. In a sense, this originally had a natural basis—that is, it was an exchange of products which Cuba easily produced and which the United States needed for products which the United States produced and Cuba needed. But it had been deformed by a series of tariff privileges for American goods that the United States had imposed upon Cuba. In this way, North American industrial products had acquired a notorious advantage over those of other countries. Naturally we opened up a little trade with the rest of the world, but under the circumstances it was far below the true potential. Sometimes it happened that Cuba had a chance to develop some crop or some product which we were buying from the United States. Then the sugar interests exerted every type of internal pressure against this production, alleging that this would affect North American interests and would occasion reprisals in the purchases of sugar (the sugar quota).

This caused the complete stagnation of our economic development. In the last thirty years before the triumph of the Revolution the population of Cuba had doubled. Yet in 1959 seven million people were living on the income from practically the same amount of sugar exports as when we were only three-and-a-half million inhabitants. An enormous unemployment developed, and—as if this were somehow related to the imbalance of trade—the North American business interests here were sending back to the United States, during the last ten years before 1959, one hundred million dollars a year more in profits than we were receiving. The little underdeveloped country was aiding the big industrialized country.

A False Image of Prosperity

If you came to Havana in those days, you saw a city with many businesses, many neon signs, lots of advertisements, many automobiles. Naturally this could have given the impression of a certain prosperity; but what it really signified was that we were spending what small resources were left to us to support an elegant life for a tiny minority of the population. Such an image of prosperity was not true of the interior of Cuba, where the people needed running water, sewers, roads, hospitals, schools, and transportation, and where hundreds of thousands of sugar workers worked only three or four months a year and lived in the most horrible social conditions imaginable. You had the paradoxical situation that those who produced the wealth were precisely the ones who least benefited from it. And the ones who spent the wealth did not live in the countryside, produced nothing, and lived a life that was soft, leisurely, easy, and proper to the wealthy. We had a wealthy class, but we didn't have a wealthy country.

That false image of prosperity, which was really the prosperity of one small class, is the image which the United States still tries to present of Cuba before the Revolution. They try to hide the true image of that epoch, the image of terrible economic and social conditions in which the vast majority of the country lived. Naturally we have not made this majority rich, but we have extraordinarily improved the conditions of their lives. We have guaranteed them medical assistance at all times, we have blotted out illiteracy, and we have offered facilities and opportunities for study to everybody, children as well as adults. Tens of thousands of housing units have been built, as well as numerous highways, roads, streets, parks, aqueducts, sewerage systems—in short, we have done everything that is within our means to improve the living conditions of this vast majority, although all this has happened to the detriment of the luxurious life which the minority led here.

For some years now we have not imported automobiles, but we have imported tens of thousands of tractors, trucks, pieces of construction equipment, etc. We are certainly not opposed to there being automobiles when the nation reaches a high level of development. But having food, shoes, clothing, medical attention, education, full employment, and sufficient housing for all the people and developing economically are far more important right now. A country cannot permit luxury to take possession while many things essential to the material and spiritual life of man have not been fulfilled.

Agriculture vs. Industry

And so by what way, along what roads, shall we set out toward the solution of our problems, the satisfaction of our needs, the growth of our economy? By investing hundreds of millions of pesos in costly industrial installations, which take years to build and to begin production, and which moreover require thousands of qualified engineers and workers, simply in order to produce some articles of which there is an excess in the world? Or else, by taking advantage of our natural resources and utilizing the hundreds of thousands of men and women capable of doing simple tasks, to begin creating wealth rapidly with a minimum of investments, producing articles of which there is a great shortage in the world?

Fruit is scarce, for example; vegetables are scarce, at least during certain times of the year; meat and milk are scarce; sugar is scarce. In short, *food* is scarce in the world, and the population of the world is growing at a rate much greater than that at which the production of foodstuffs increases. Consequently, a country that develops the production of foodstuffs along scientific lines, as our country is able to do, will be producing something for which there is an unlimited need. To the degree that numerous areas of the world become more and more industrialized, the position of the food-producing countries improves, because it is easier for an industralized country to produce an automobile than to produce a bull.

What is happening in Europe? Industry is well developed, the workers earn relatively high wages, many of them have refrigerators, television sets, record players, washing machines, tape recorders, even automobiles. Nevertheless, they want to eat more meat, which is very expensive and often beyond the reach of their wages; they want to eat more fruit, more vegetables; they want to improve their diet. Moreover, the Socialist countries are now achieving an extraordinary industrial development. But at the same time their full employment and social development have brought about an enormous need for food. If we add to these all of the underdeveloped countries, such as Egypt, Morocco, and others, which are trying to develop their economies, it can be clearly seen that everything we are able to produce in agriculture has a market.

So we have come to the conclusion that our main source of immediate returns lies in agriculture, in which we must invest our present resources while we are preparing the people and developing our general and technical education. This means that until the year 1970 we will devote ourselves fundamentally to the development of agriculture. Then, from 1970 to 1980, we will proceed to the development of other lines of industry which require a higher level of technique and investment. . . .

Economic Development

LOCKWOOD: From the time you came to power in 1959 until just recently you were following a policy of crash industrialization and deemphasizing agriculture. Why did you suddenly change your mind about industrializing and decide to push agricultural development again?

CASTRO: The problem of industrialization, as a generic concept, has been used as a slogan by nearly all underdeveloped countries. It would be clearer and more exact to speak of *economic* development, because it is a more complete term that includes both agricultural and industrial development. The possibilities I have just been explaining are the result of analyzing the experiences of that period. We didn't know them, and really we couldn't know them then; the conditions which existed in 1959 for our trade, our conditions for markets, were radically different from those of today. At that time, the greater part of our trade was still with the United States, and our economy was tightly interwoven with the North American economy. In those days we were, practically speaking, wholly ignorant of the enormous market possibilities that we had in the Socialist camp, even though there was tied to the slogan of industrialization another slogan, also vague and generic, which other countries are still using today: "extensive trade with all the nations of the world."

Naturally, "extensive trade with all the nations of the

world" was something that would have clashed directly with the interests of the United States. Also, in those days everybody talked about the Revolution, about structural changes, and naturally those changes in social structure were also going to clash with the interests of the United States. At that time the United States didn't talk about agrarian reform; at that time the United States didn't talk about structural changes. That is, they didn't speak about land reform, tax reform, or about social development. That is a language the United States began to use some years later, out of the fear that new revolutions like the one in Cuba might break out in Latin America.

We were speaking in vague and generic terms about "industrialization," "wide trade," "revolution." Today, these ideas have been made more clear, concrete, and real: structural change that is full and profound; economic development along the road of our agriculture; priority in this period to those branches of industry which serve as a basis for a modern agriculture; an educational plan of enormous breadth for the preparation of technicians for agriculture and industry, without which economic and social development are impossible.

The Importance of Land Management

LOCKWOOD: Would you say that the leaders of the Revolution made many mistakes during those first years?

CASTRO: We made many mistakes, many small mistakes, but no serious errors whose consequences might endure for a long time. That is, whenever we have taken a false step, we have been able to correct it immediately.

Could we have avoided making mistakes? I think not. Not to make mistakes would have meant anticipating each situation perfectly before it came up. That was absolutely impossible.

Now then, I am going to give you an example of what could have been a grave mistake in agriculture.

At the beginning of the Revolution, if we had followed the classic path which other countries have followed, we would have divided up the land. This would have been a mistake of such transcendence that its consequences would have been felt for a long time. You will remember that even in my Moncada speech, "History Will Absolve Me," and also when I was in the Sierra Maestra, I spoke not about dividing up the land but rather of organizing cooperatives— large enterprises of production in a cooperative form.

I found upon the victory of the Revolution that the idea of land division still had a lot of currency. But I already understood by then that if you take, for example, a sugar plantation of twenty-five hundred acres where the land is good for sugar cane, in the vicinity of a sugar mill, and you divide it into two hundred portions of twelve-and-a-half acres each, what will inevitably happen is that right away the new owners will cut the production of sugar cane in half in each plot, and they will begin to raise for their own consumption a whole series of crops for which in many cases the soil will not be adequate. Accordingly, if we had undertaken that kind of agrarian reform, dividing up the land, we would have mortgaged the agricultural future of our country, and none of the agricultural projects could have been carried out, as we are now doing, using the land in the most practical way, utilizing machinery, irrigation, fertilization, and technology on a large scale. The small landowner produces primarily for his own sustenance. And that is why small landowning is not the answer for providing food for the dietary needs of a population with a decently high standard of living. The only way to meet those needs is by the use of machinery to the greatest possible degree, and by employing fertilization, irrigation, and all the techniques which permit intensive production. This can be achieved only through the kind of management where the machine, the labor force, and technology are employed in an optimum, rational way. That is the concept of the *granja*, or "people's farm.". . .

The People's Farm

LOCKWOOD: What exactly is a people's farm?

CASTRO: It's an agricultural production center whose

lands are the property of the nation and which is operated as an enterprise of the nation.

I will give you a more concrete example. The United Fruit Company owned some three hundred and twenty-five thousand acres of land. Its stockholders lived in the United States and received a profit there, an income, without ever having visited those lands. The company assigned an administrator—naturally they tried to assign a good one—who ran things like a huge agricultural enterprise. Today, the substantial difference is that there are no foreign stockholders who own the business and receive the profits. Today, the enterprise belongs to the nation, which uses its profits for economic and social development for all—for schools, hospitals, roads, housing for workers, the acquisition of machinery, etc.

Thus, our success consists in having a good organization, designating good administrative groups, with a further advantage that the North American company could not have. The North American company was in constant social conflict with the workers, while the *granja* acts in permanent cooperation with the workers, who have their party organizations, their union organizations, their youth organizations, their women's organizations, who work there, who study, who receive the greater part of the profits and many benefits they did not receive before, who have the possibility of progressing in accordance with their level of experience and preparation, since from their own ranks come the men who occupy the posts of management and of responsibility.

And this also allows us to introduce mechanization. The company could not introduce mechanization. Why? Because there was a lot of unemployment in the country. If they had gone ahead and put in a machine to cut the sugar cane, the workers would not have permitted it, because that would have meant a shortening of the three or four months of the year in which they worked, a reduction of their incomes. Today, since there is work for all, no laborer fears the machine or looks upon it as an enemy, but on the contrary he sees the machine as a friend, because he is changed from a manual worker to a mechanical worker who is going to have better living conditions, more income, and easier work.

Finally, the company had to limit production because the country had limited markets. It had no reason for introducing fertilizers, irrigation, or methods of extensive production. Today, we are able to apply all these methods and increase production as much as we want, because we have the markets. We maintain full employment, and at the same time we considerably improve the living conditions of the workers and their families.

The Persistence of Private Farms

Alongside the system of people's farms there still exists the system of small landowners who own their own farms. The small farmers can hold up to one hundred and sixty acres of land. Of course in a country like Japan one hundred and sixty acres would be considered a vast estate, but in Cuba they are considered small farms. Also, there are some exceptions made for very efficient farmers who have always completely fulfilled their obligations to the state. Under the policy adopted by the Second Agrarian Reform Law toward the most competent, dependable, and hard-working farmers, there are some unusual cases of holdings up to nine hundred acres.

The Revolutionary Government sustains these individual landowners, it gives them credit and resources and buys their surplus produce, whatever they do not need for their own consumption. They can even sell individually, provided it is not in wholesale quantities. A neighbor who wants to buy from them, individual people, thus can go and buy.

Obviously, there are some exceptions. A product like sugar cane, which requires an industrial process, can only be bought by the sugar mill. But many other things, like eggs, chickens, and milk, can be traded freely on a small scale. Sales in large amounts are made only by the state.

LOCKWOOD: There is a limit on how much they may sell?

CASTRO: They cannot sell over a certain quantity in each case. They can sell to any family as much as they wish to buy for their own consumption.

What happened, for example, with regard to eggs? Before, when production was limited, the small farmers sold eggs at an exorbitant price, at thirty cents an egg. When the government's program of egg production was developed, the price was reduced to six, seven, and eight cents. They can now consume the eggs they produce or sell them at that price, which is a fair one. The best way to fight speculation, in our experience, is not by taking measures of a legal nature, but by increasing production.

Although some small farmers have organized their own cooperatives, we do not exert pressure on them to do so. In fact, we are not even interested in organizing them into cooperatives. Why? First of all, out of respect for their traditions, for their habits as small individual property owners. Any effort to organize cooperatives could have clashed in part with those feelings. Second, because we believe that with the passage of time every one of these small farms will progressively become a part of the National Common Lands Fund. How? Through expropriation? No. Through new agrarian reforms? No; we have promised them that the era of agrarian reform laws is already ended. How, then? By buying the land whenever there is a farmer who wishes to sell out.

There are cases of farmers whose children go into the army or who are away studying in schools or in technological institutes. They have been left completely alone, and some of them are old. So they want to sell out. There are other cases of farmers who grow too old for farm work and want to retire. When such cases have come to our attention, we have bought the land and given them a pension. The possibility of selling his farm and receiving a pension besides is one of the incentives that allows us to go on acquiring new lands. But in no case is any pressure ever applied. His right to his piece of land will be respected absolutely.

Government Policy Toward Small Farmers

LOCKWOOD: How many small farmers are there in Cuba now?

CASTRO: There must be, I believe, some one hundred

and fifty thousand, counting the smallest. But actually, considering only those with any kind of economic productivity, I figure that there must be around one hundred thousand.

At present, seventy percent of the land is nationalized, thirty percent is privately owned. It does not matter to us if within twenty years twenty percent of the land is privately owned, if within forty years ninety percent is nationalized and ten percent is privately owned. It doesn't matter how long it takes. It will be a completely evolutionary process.

LOCKWOOD: Do small farmers have the same privileges as those who work for the state—medical care, scholarships for their children, and so forth?

CASTRO: Yes, and they have that right without any kind of discrimination. Indisputably, the owner of one hundred or one hundred and fifty acres of land has a larger income than a farm laborer, but nothing would be gained by establishing a different system with regard for social services—for example, to charge for education, to charge for medical care—because the nation socially benefits from having the children of small farmers study and become technicians. Furthermore, the Revolution has established free education and medical care for all citizens. Politically and socially, it wouldn't be right to exclude them, and it wouldn't be conducive to educating the new generations of those farmers in socialism.

Formerly, you must realize, those small farmers were exploited. They paid rent, they received very low prices for their produce, they were charged high interest rates on loans, they had no roads or schools or hospitals. The Revolution has freed them from paying any rent, it has offered them many benefits, and it has given them ease of mind by promising that there will be no new measures of an agrarian nature for them. This creates the conditions for the union of the *campesinos* with the Revolutionary Government. It is very important to follow a correct policy toward the farmers, because the power of the Revolution is based on the intimate union of the workers and peasants.

Our belief that we have resolved this problem correctly is borne out by the fact that the counterrevolution has not been able to penetrate the mass of farmers. Of course there are always exceptions of individual peasants or workers who are won over by the counterrevolution, just as many people of the middle class have been won over by the Revolution. But essentially the support of the Revolution among the farming and working sections is very great, and I believe that as the years pass it will become greater and greater, better organized, and more efficient.

Taking a Stand Against Imperialism

Fidel Castro

The greatest obstacle the Cuban Revolution had to overcome was the active opposition and interference of the United States. Outraged that American citizens had lost millions of dollars' worth of investments in Cuba after Fidel Castro nationalized them, the U.S. government did everything in its power to prevent the revolution from succeeding. In 1961 it backed an invasion of the island at Playa Girón (the Bay of Pigs) by Cuban exiles. When this invasion was repulsed, the United States initiated the Alliance for Progress with other Latin American nations. The purpose of the alliance was to provide massive U.S. financial aid to these nations so that they could improve the living conditions of their citizens. One condition of the aid, however, was that recipient nations must cut all ties, diplomatic and commercial, with Cuba. By greatly reducing trade between Cuba and its closest trading partners, the United States hoped to cripple the Castro regime's ability to build socialism on the island.

This excerpt is from a speech made by Castro in 1966 on the fifth anniversary of the attempted invasion at Playa Girón. In it he outlines some of the progress the revolution has achieved, and some of the internal obstacles it still faces. He also acknowledges that "Yankee imperialism" continues to be Cuba's greatest problem, and warns that future invasions of the island will meet with concerted opposition by the Cuban people.

Our Revolution and our people stand firm against imperialist power, its political influence, its long experience
in aggression, crime, subversion, and piracy—an experience
with which many peoples of other continents are also
familiar. And that is a task for revolutionaries, for genuine
revolutionaries.

And if our people have taken that road, it is because they
are capable of following such a road, in that historic mission
which has fallen to our country in this epoch. Our country,
the last to free itself from the Spanish colonial yoke—since
the other nations of this Continent preceded us by almost a
century—waged alone its battle in the heroic Ten Years' War
and in the War for Independence, and carried on armed
struggle for almost thirty years to achieve an independence
which was stolen from us at the last minute. But to our
country belongs the glory of being the first to achieve its
second and true independence.

Legacy of Yankee Imperialism

That this is clearly true is shown by the example of Santo
Domingo, militarily occupied by Yankee troops,[1] in the same
style that they might occupy any farm or *latifundium* [plan-
tation], as if they were the lords and masters of this Continent. We see this truth in the history of the Central American countries—in the history, for example, of Guatemala,
whose revolutionary government was liquidated by a Girón-
type aggression with the complicity of a Batista-type army.

We see it in the situation of almost all the countries of
South America where the United States removes and sets up
governments at will; countries unable to say, as we do, that
they have achieved definite independence; countries which,
having freed themselves from Spain a century and a half
ago, spent one hundred years working mainly for the English imperialists, or rather for European imperialism, and

---

1. In 1965 the United States sent thirty thousand troops to the Dominican Republic (aka
Santo Domingo) to prevent a supposedly pro-Castro leftist movement from overthrowing
the conservative military regime in power. The troops remained until 1966, when the conservatives defeated the leftists in a presidential election.

another half-century working for Yankee imperialism. One hundred and fifty years of history!

And while many nations were developing, were becoming industrialized, our Latin American nations straggled behind and became poorer and poorer. And the gap separating the industrialized countries from Latin America grew wider. Population also grew. But resources, wealth, and industry did not grow; the population increased more than did food production.

A hundred and fifty years of accumulated misery! During that century and a half, Cuba spent one hundred years toiling and struggling to free herself from Spanish colonialism. And then during more than half a century, we worked for the Yankee imperialists, the corrupt politicians, and the privileged few who squandered the resources of this country for almost sixty years.

They build few factories. The privileged of this country and the corrupt politicians bought country estates, built mansions, deposited millions in foreign banks. And meanwhile, in the countryside, the men who cut the cane and produced the sugar, the men who, in other words, produced the country's foreign exchange, lived in huts and hovels. They never saw cement, nor electric lights, nor running water, nor streets, nor parks. They worked for such a long time and received such an insignificant share of the national product, while our capital city grew and grew. A drive along Fifth Avenue [a fashionable residential street in Havana] is sufficient to see where a good part of the sweat of the workers of this country was invested.

And undoubtedly we are making the best possible use of those palatial mansions; it is a fact that today we have tens of thousands of students living in those houses. But what we lack are cement factories; what we lack are fertilizer factories; what they did not leave us were industries, except for a few entirely dependent upon imported raw materials, and the sugar mills, the newest of which is more than thirty years old, because in the last thirty years not a single new sugar mill has been built. And many of those industries are old and almost dilapidated.

They did not even leave us an advanced mechanized agriculture. They did not, nor could they, because the workers had opposed mechanization, since under capitalism the introduction of machinery is opposed by the workers as it takes away their jobs and leaves them to starve. Neither cane-loading machines, nor cane harvesters, nor cane-conditioning centers, nor bulk loading facilities; not one of these modern labor-saving techniques would they have been able to introduce into our country.

The Unity of Labor and Resources

Today, the fight of our country is for the introduction of those techniques. It does not occur to anyone in this country today to consider a machine his enemy. Today, when there is total identification of the people with their resources; today, when there is complete identification of the laborer with the fruits of his labor; today, when hundreds of thousands of men and women mobilize to increase production, it would not occur to anyone to consider a machine his enemy. For that reason, capitalism and imperialism left us a backward agriculture. They could neither introduce machines, nor did they need to introduce machines. For cutting cane, they counted on the immense army of seasonally unemployed who anxiously awaited the harvest months in order to pay off the debts they had contracted during the dead season and eat enough to survive. There was an abundance of cheap labor.

And when the workers got together to make demands, seeking improvements in their miserable living conditions, there was the rural guard. For it must be said that those soldiers of the privileged class also knew how to handle the machete, but not exactly to cut cane; they knew how to handle the machete to beat the farmers, the workers, the unfortunate.

What a difference! And how can this difference be understood by those who are accustomed to seeing that the role of weapons has been to defend the powerful, the privileged, and the rich? The imperialists are accustomed to creating armies of parasites to serve the exploiters and, when have they ever seen an army wield the machete to cut cane, to work, to produce, to increase the wealth of the people? How could they ever understand the power of the Revolution?

Building Anew

In our countryside, there still exists much of the poverty they left us. But it is a fact that there is no longer a dead season. That affliction has disappeared from our country forever: the dead season has died.

It is a fact that there is practically not a single corner of our country without a school, nor is there a region of our country without a hospital. We are now, in education as well as in medical care, without doubt the foremost country of this continent, including the U.S.

But there is still much poverty; there still exist many inadequate dwellings. Thousands of kilometers of roads and hundreds of thousands of houses must be built, as well as electrical installations and water supplies. And that, naturally, cannot be achieved in a few years, especially in a country that produces about one-third of the cement it could use at this time.

And before the Revolution there was an excess of cement which, naturally, was not employed in building highways in the mountains, nor bridges in the interior of the country, because when they built a highway, it was like the Via Blanca, that is, a highway that crosses regions where there is practically no agriculture, and that leads from Havana to Varadero [a beach popular with wealthy havanistas]. Did they ever build a highway all the way to Baracoa, as the Revolution has done, with constructions that are truly impressive because of the technical solutions devised for the laying of a highway over such difficult terrain? Were highways like that constructed before in the province of Oriente? Of course not! Rural housing programs? Unheard of!

A large part of the cement produced in this country was used for building weekend country homes. Today the supply of cement is insufficient. And although some cement is imported, it is still not enough. Everyone needs cement—

all the municipal governments and everyone else—not just those dedicated to public works but those in agriculture and in water projects as well. Everywhere we hear the same thing: "We need cement." And unfortunately cement factories cannot be built in a few weeks. Our new cement factories—the first being built in Nuevitas, the second in Las Villas, and the Santiago de Cuba plant is being enlarged—will double our cement production. However, even when our cement production has been doubled, what are two million tons of cement for our needs? A third factory is already being considered. To begin to solve part of our problem, we must necessarily plan to double, triple, or quadruple the amount of cement that we have today.

The road is long and patience is needed. This is the road of any underdeveloped country. But at least since the triumph of the Revolution, well done or not, better or worse, our work no longer benefits the foreigner. We no longer work for a privileged class. Even though it has been necessary to create everything, to begin everything from zero, it was necessary to overthrow the rotting bourgeois state in order to build anew. The country had to be completely revolutionized. It was necessary to do away with the old and to rebuild. And this task had to be carried out with new men, the great majority of whom lacked experience.

Creating Legions of Technicians

Our country suffered from a true poverty of technical personnel. And part of the technical personnel—of what little technical personnel this country had—was identified with the interests affected by the Revolution. It was necessary to begin to prepare cadres. And this also takes years. In spite of the efforts made, legions of new technicians have not yet entered production; it will take us a few years but we will get there. We will reach the goal because we have not wasted time, having set about this task from the very beginning. In some activities in some fields, tens of thousands are already prepared. The triumph of the Revolution found almost 10,000 unemployed teachers. All those teachers were given jobs and this did not solve the problem. There weren't enough teachers. Special courses had to be organized in order to send teachers to the mountains and there were still not enough.

Last year almost one thousand teachers were graduated from our Pedagogical Institute. Part of these went to the mountains to replace the teachers who had spent five years in this service and those left were too few to fill the needs. The workers' technological institutes needed teachers and the Army needed teachers, too.

Thousands of soldiers are studying in accelerated courses, because as our military techniques increase and modernize, the knowledge needed also increases. There are not enough teachers. These thousands of men need teachers, as do the thousands of workers who study in the technological institutes and as also do practically all the factories of the country, all the state farms. But there are not enough teachers. Nevertheless, more than 20,000 young men and women are in teacher-training schools. And we do not want to rush them, we do not want to interrupt their studies to solve immediate problems; we prefer to wait until they have acquired sufficient preparation to be the kind of teachers that we want to produce. An enormous effort is being made in agriculture, but our agriculture also lacks an adequate number of technicians. Nevertheless, approximately 20,000 students are enrolled in our agricultural technological institutes.

Before 1970, those 20,000 will have graduated, as will more than 20,000 teachers, and, in addition, by 1970, we shall have some 30,000 new students being trained as teachers, and another 30,000 students in the agricultural technological institutes. That is, our country is moving forward with a huge number of people who are receiving training precisely in order to regain the ground lost during more than a century and in order to attain levels of economic development which we had not been able to reach before.

Where do we stand today? We strive to have the greatest possible number of young people in our universities. If 10,000 enroll, it seems few to us; if 20,000 enroll, they are still too few. Nevertheless, when one reads the news reports about the situation in the universities in other countries of Latin America, the case is different. The number of university students is limited, and problems exist in many countries of Latin America because of this limitation on the number of students who can enter the universities. What future can these economically underdeveloped, technically backward countries have if they close the doors of their universities? For not only do the university graduates have difficulties in getting jobs, but a large number of them emigrate to the United States seeking employment. How can these countries overcome their underdevelopment and their poverty if they close the doors of their universities?

Who can know this better than we? Who can better understand the enormous need for technicians?

We Work to Satisfy the Needs of the People

Of course a social system which is totally unconcerned with the health of its people does not need many doctors. In countries where practically no medical service exists, there are more than enough doctors, who always tend to concentrate in the big cities.

In countries full of large land-holdings, where agriculture is under feudal-type regime, agronomists are not needed, veterinarians are not needed, mechanical engineers are not needed.

Our need for mechanical engineers is constantly present. Why? Because the need constantly arises for machines, machines of every kind: machines for fertilizing, clearing, and cultivating; machines for cutting, cleaning, and transporting sugar cane. And our need for mechanical engineers is evident; our need for hydraulic engineers is evident; for civil engineers, electrical engineers, architects, chemists, and research workers. Our need for pedagogues, university professors, professors for pre-university and technological institutes, our need for skilled workers in industry, in production, for the development of the country, for the fulfilling of its social needs, is constantly arising. Because that is precisely the task of the Revolution; to develop the country in every way, to develop the country materially and culturally.

In our system no one works to make profits for any individual; we work to satisfy the needs of the people, to enrich the country, to raise the productivity of labor; every citizen of this country is today concerned with increasing labor productivity; every citizen in this country is, logically, interested in raising and multiplying the productivity of a rural worker, of a caneworker, of a construction worker, of a mineworker, a transport worker, a fisherman, because our resources will increase and it will be possible to take care of the most pressing needs of the people in the same measure as labor productivity increases.

These are the things that make our case different from that of the other Latin American nations. We are ahead of them. And in a world where the population increases more rapidly than the output of foodstuffs, how will the underdeveloped nations be able to face this tremendous problem without Revolution, without doing precisely what we are doing?

Today, for example, some press reports mention the five years of the "Alliance for Progress." The "Alliance for Progress," is, in part, a result of the imperialist defeat at Playa Girón. The "Alliance for Progress" appeared after Playa Girón. The imperialists decided to set up a program which—they said—was aimed at solving the problems of Latin America so that no more revolutions such as Cuba's would take place.

Faulty Imperialist Remedies

But what remedies does imperialism wish to apply to those ills? It seeks to apply imperialist remedies, capitalist remedies. And, logically, imperialist remedies cannot be remedies at all, because it was precisely imperialist remedies that led those countries into the present state of affairs.

But they said they were going to lend money to build roads, schools, waterworks, and housing, and at the same time that the "good and noble" U.S. investors were going to invest money in these countries to develop their economies.

And today, the press stories have it that up to now the

"Alliance for Progress" had been a disappointment but, nevertheless, certain amounts had been invested. And they said, for example, that the United States had lent 5,000 million dollars; that, in addition, private investors had invested 9,000 million dollars in Latin America, and that the respective governments had invested an indefinite number of thousands of millions of dollars.

But they said that a good deal of the money lent had been squandered, that some of the "Alliance for Progress" aid had been used, in a country like Brazil, to buy things such as confetti for Christmas—confetti are tiny pieces of paper that are tossed. I suppose that confetti is not the same as "confite" [sweets] that is today, money spent on trivial things.

They also reported that some governments had said they were going to make some reforms, but that the reforms they had made were very few. Yet the following was the most interesting part: that sixty percent of the aid had been loaned to pay back foreign debts, in other words, that sixty out of each hundred dollars of that so-called aid given by the imperialists was destined to pay debts to those same imperialists and to contract new debts with them.

And it was precisely the dispatches of the Yankee news agencies which spoke of the failure of the "Alliance for Progress," and many Latin American governments of the servile type, unconditional supporters of imperialism, are evidently so disillusioned that at every meeting of the representatives of those governments they seem to have gotten together for the purpose of asking, requesting, and demanding help, stating that practically no help has been given them.

Many of them give examples of what the imperialists do: they lend one dollar and then cut the price two dollars on the products that they buy from Latin America.

The imperialists possess what they call strategic reserves of copper, tin, of various products, and every now and then they dump these reserves on the market. When it's tin, Bolivia collapses. When it's copper, the bottom falls out of Chile, and so on. When they're not doing this, they dump great stocks of cotton, causing crises in half a dozen cotton-exporting countries, and so on.

Cuba's Case Is Different

Five years have elapsed since Girón. Naturally, we have difficulties; we have a difficult road to travel. This is evident. But at least we're moving forward: we work for the future; we face all these difficulties and we are sure that we are going to overcome them.

Five years after Girón, the other countries of Latin America admit their defeat, their disillusionment, their pessimism. What happens in those countries does not happen in Cuba. In those countries people work so that a minority of the population may eat well, and very well indeed, while the rest must shift for themselves.

In those countries there is no rationing, because there is another traditional type of rationing: unemployment and a lack of purchasing power among the masses. In those countries when an item becomes scarce, its price doubles or triples or quadruples or quintuples, and then the workers, or the sectors of the population which have limited resources, can buy absolutely nothing, while the rich minorities can buy absolutely anything they want.

This is taken care of by the law of supply and demand: when there is a scarcity of any item, the masses must do without it.

We have a different situation because we consider it necessary to attend to the needs of every citizen. It is true that we have rationing, and we will have it on certain items for a few more years, but nobody in this country can say that he doesn't have the money to buy what is allotted to him on the rationing card. If anyone does say that, it's of his own free choice: it means that he doesn't want to work.

There is work of one type or another for everyone. The Revolutionary State has never denied assistance to any family with problems. There is not one single family in this country that can say it is neglected, at least not after having gone to ask for help from the Revolution.

Revolutionary Solidarity

And when we say the Cuban Revolution, we are speaking of the Revolution in Latin America. And when we speak of the revolution in Latin America we are speaking of revolution on a universal scale, the revolution of the peoples of Asia, Africa and of Europe. Here, as a symbol of what this Revolution means and what the other revolutions of other heroic peoples mean, we have a delegation from the heroic people of Korea, whose outstanding leader Comrade Kim-Il Sung, sent today a very friendly message of solidarity, for the celebration of the victory of Girón. Kim-Il-Sung is one of the most distinguished, brilliant, and heroic socialist leaders in the world today, and his story, perhaps, because he is the leader of a small nation, is not sufficiently known. It is one of the most splendid stories that a revolutionary has written in the cause of socialism.

For us this message of solidarity has extraordinary value, because Korea, in the same way as the heroic people of Viet Nam, knows what the imperialists are. Just as the people of Viet Nam are doing today, the people of Korea also heroically faced the armies of Yankee imperialism and inflicted severe defeats upon them.

Our nation has good examples to follow in the peoples of Korea and Viet Nam. They are heroic peoples, heroic Parties, which in spite of their small geographic size have confronted the imperialist monster and have written pages of extraordinary heroism.

We are not denying the heroism of any people. The heroic peoples of the world are many, both of large and small nations. But naturally we look with great sympathy upon those men who at a given hour taught the peoples of the world that, regardless of size, it is possible to fight against the imperialists and to withstand the imperialists' aggressions.

The imperialists are cowards. They like to be merciless with small nations, while at the same time they tremble at the possibility of coming to blows with the great powers.

In the United States there are many senators and leaders who talk every day about aggressions against Cuba and invasions of Cuba, because they imagine they are going to have "easy pickings" here. And really, we are not interested in persuading them to the contrary.

Defeating Aggression

We know that aggressions are not defeated by words but by weapons. We know that we are not going to save ourselves from the dangers of an invasion by scaring the imperialists. We confront the dangers of an invasion, or the consequences of any invasion, by preparing ourselves, constantly preparing ourselves! And we will not stop preparing ourselves for one single minute.

I said that there wasn't enough cement, that the resources we require are many, but nevertheless, the country does not scrimp on the resources channeled into defense. It does not scrimp on the resources that it channels into strengthening the Revolution. And therefore I said that we do not seek to frighten the imperialists, because that would be ridiculous. And it is without any desire to frighten when I say that they are going to find a very hard bone to gnaw here. We know this, because they will have to face the entire people everywhere, everywhere! Because if the imperialists believe that with the swarm of parasites that they have there they could get this country moving they are mistaken! If they believe that with that plague of parasites they are going to cut the sugar cane of this country, and get their transport, industries, mines, and agriculture on the move with those who have never sweated their shirts, no! When they bring in all that plague, supposing that they do arrive, supposing they got in, and supposing that they had one whole stone, left to sit on, supposing all this, then on top of everything they would say to the Yankees: "Good, now send us some maids." Because if the day should come when the Yankees had them installed here in some houses (which would have to be imaginary), on top of everything else they would ask for some maids because they have never soaked a shirt with sweat.

Ah! but those who cut cane, those who work, those who create with their hands, those who make this country move by their work, all these, all, will be wielding something, but not tools to work for the imperialists, but weapons to kill them! And here, if the imperialists set foot in this country, the first decree will be that decree, like Bolívar's,[1] which declared war to the death against the enemy. And there won't be one healthy imperialist's head left within reach of our hands. Pilots who bomb here, pilots who drop a bomb on this country might as well commit *hara-kiri* [suicide] in the air, because they are not going to last even three minutes on the ground. If the imperialists should one day bomb this country, if the imperialists should set foot in this country, they will learn that there will not be any imperialist prisoners around here; none will escape; the first decree will be, like the decree of Bolívar in the struggle for independence, a war to the death against every imperialist or puppet-imperialist enemy that may tread this land.

And today, on the Fifth Anniversary of Girón, when we have come here to commemorate the victory and to pay tribute to the memory of our dead, there is no better day than this to tell our enemies what awaits them, and that the generosity of Girón will not be repeated, neither with mercenary invaders nor with imperialist invaders, because we do not want war, we do not want the destruction of our wealth, we do not want the destruction of the fruits of our labor, but if they touch a single hair of ours, a single hair, they will have to kill us all, down to the last revolutionary citizen of this country, because we know that pirates have to be dealt with as pirates, that bandits have to be dealt with as bandits.

And we are a small country but against this country, against its dignity, against its integrity . . . this country which is the first one to conquer true independence, the vanguard of America, an example for all the other countries of this Continent; this country which defies imperialism and all its might and marches forward, does so because it is ready to do so, because it is ready to march ahead, because it is certain that it will march ahead, because no one

1. Simon Bolívar liberated much of South America from Spanish rule.

can prevent us from doing so. And if they attack us, they will be smashed by that integrity and that heroism. Because we will be martyrs, like those of Girón, rather than the slaves of anyone!

Patria o Muerte! Venceremos! ["Fatherland or death! We shall vanquish!" (the mottoes of the Cuban Revolution).]

Creating "Fidel's Utopia"

Andrew Salkey

The revolution changed the lives of working Cubans in myr-
iad ways, usually for the better. Before the revolution, hundreds of thousands of workers, especially sugar cane cutters,
were unemployed for more than half the year. Their wages
were kept low by the foreign corporations, and they could
expect no redress from a government that cooperated with the
corporations. After the revolution, seasonal unemployment
virtually ceased, and the wages of all workers were increased.
In addition, the government implemented a number of social
security programs to improve the lot of the working-class
Cuban.

Andrew Salkey, a Jamaican novelist, attended a cultural
congress in Havana in January 1968. During his stay he
toured the island and interviewed a number of ordinary
Cubans. In this excerpt, he talks with an unidentified student
of political science in Havana about the future of "Fidel's
Utopia." The student tells Salkey about the tremendous
improvements the revolution has made for most Cubans, and
confesses to his belief that things will only continue to get
better with time.

Salkey: Let's begin with the Trades Union movement. All
right by you?

Student: Before that, I'd like to say that we've got in Cuba
what we call Labour Courts, which are constituted of five

Andrew Salkey, *Havana Journal*. New York: Penguin Books, 1971. Copyright © 1971 by
Andrew Salkey. Reproduced by permission.

workers, selected by co-workers themselves in a secret ballot. These are very effective.

Salkey: How do they work?

Student: Well, a Court hears a case of serious grievance, or it may be just an ordinary complaint, between worker and worker, or between worker and management, and decides in the particular case and has the authority to do so. It can also settle other more complex disputes to do with social security matters.

Salkey: And the Unions?

Student: We've got a Union movement. Naturally.

Salkey: Why do you say 'naturally'?

Student: We've always had Unions in Cuba. There's a tradition, so to speak. That's what I meant. The whole thing was totally different, of course. Besides, our Revolutionary Labour policy demands that we have a Union movement. I must tell you that the old system has been completely revolutionized. Unjust resolutions, rigged internal elections and so on are finished. And where the worker himself is immediately concerned, things are also very different. No more wrongful dismissals and social inequalities. One of the first things we did after the Revolution was to secure the freedom of all workers in Cuba to organize themselves into strong Unions for the logical protection of their labour rights and other rights too, and for the good of the country as a whole, for basic production and for progressive production. You know that we've just had a big Trades Union Congress, the twelfth one? The C.T.C. (Central Union of Cuban Workers) is going ahead with new plans. It's the umbrella organization, if you like, for the country's unionized workers and it's working out problems very well, so far.

Salkey: What's the C.T.C.'s job?

Student: Well, it organizes, sets up really, the Unions throughout Cuba, for the workers of all kinds, professors and manual workers. It sees to their interests. It helps to achieve greater production. It is there to strengthen Socialism, really, and to educate the workers and to redistribute the different Unions in the country into new groupings. Did you know that we had twenty-five Unions once, and we have fourteen now?

Salkey: How does the work of the C.T.C. affect the Unions directly?

Student: The C.T.C. isn't a bureaucratic luxury. It isn't at all. The C.T.C. gives advice, expert advice, and makes progressive studies, detailed studies of all the aspects of Unionism in the country. Any of our National Unions can call on the C.T.C. for immediate advice. We had a lot to correct where our labour policy and the lives of the workers were concerned. We've done all that in a fairly short time too, I think.

Increasing Wages

Salkey: How about wages?

Student: Well, first of all, you know that you think of our peso as what?

Salkey: A dollar? Seven shillings, approximately, maybe?

Student: Yes. Well, I think in pesos, you see, and in dollars too. We were in a terrible way before the Revolution. Nearly twenty-five per cent of the labour force used to be unemployed, ten years ago. That would be like, I don't know, about six hundred thousand people? In those days, nearly two thirds of the working people earned something like seventy pesos or so a month.

Salkey: What about the skilled people? The technicians and the highly qualified labour force?

Student: They got more, yes. A little better than starvation wages. But the other side of the picture, the workers on seasonal crop-work, about two hundred and fifty thousand, three hundred and fifty thousand of them were the lowest paid and very badly off. No protection. Exploited. Abused. Cheated all the time. And most of the time out of work, too. But the urban workers were sometimes much worse off, what with the very high cost of living in the city, taxes, criminal rents and things like school fees and doctor's bills and, in many instances, no pension scheme whatsoever. They even had to accept very, very low wages, outside the law, at that. The law meant nothing to employers. They controlled the Labour Unions then. Bribed officials and the rest of it. The worker had no protection at all.

Salkey: And wages now?

Student: That was done like this. The real wage-grading, as a consequence of many national reductions and basic cuts in all sorts of things, like rents, education, medical care and many other things; as a result of those things, the Revolutionary Government saved the people about ninety million pesos all round. So you see the wages are better everywhere by quite a substantial rise and the expenses are almost not in existence any more. They are nil in many areas of the workers' lives. You must remember that we are struggling at the moment, and therefore our wage-system may not look

Rehabilitating Political Prisoners

Although those who were suspected of being hard-core counterrevolutionaries were imprisoned under harsh conditions, most political prisoners were not. These people, most of whom were politically naïve peasants, were confined in work camps where an attempt was made to rehabilitate them. In his 1967 book subtitled An American Journalist's Inside Look at Today's Cuba, *Lee Lockwood describes the rehabilitation efforts.*

One class which every prisoner attends is called "political studies." This is basically a course in Cuban history, together with a smattering of elementary economics and sociology, all taught from a stridently Marxist theoretical point of view. The texts, which I have had an opportunity to study, are identical with those used for political science instruction in the armed forces. They contain liberal doses of Marx, Engels, and Lenin, as well as speeches and theoretical writings by leading Cuban Communists, including, of course, Fidel Castro. . . .

To each barracks there is assigned a "revolutionary instructor" from the Ministry of the Interior, the agency responsible for all of Cuba's prisons. This man, who eats, sleeps, and lives with his charges, is carefully selected for attractive to someone from the developed industrialized world, but the old wage-system has been bettered considerably, and the excessive burdens on the individual worker have been lifted clear off his shoulders. Yes, there has been a moderate rise in wages and an enormous helping hand from the State is helping to make the moderate rise a true economic increment.

Eliminating Unemployment

Salkey: Unemployment?

Student: In the provinces of Cuba, the rural provinces, none. None whatsoever. In fact, do you know that the work opportunities are so great in the country areas that paid workers and volunteer workers from Havana have to go

his intelligence and understanding. Often, he is himself a former peasant. He is to his men a combined barracks sergeant, ideological mentor, and father-figure to whom they bring all their problems. It is his main responsibility to mark each prisoner's progress, and it is primarily his reports which determine when a man is ready to return to the outside.

A prisoner may be eligible for release after serving at least one year in the plan and a minimum of twenty-five percent of his total sentence. Exactly how much longer he serves depends on his conduct, his work record, and his progress in developing a "neutral," i.e., positive, attitude toward the Revolution.

In order not to create jealousy among the other prisoners, a *reeducando* about to be released is not so informed until the night before he is to leave. Then he is issued a suit of new clothes and some "mustering-out" pay and wished good luck by the authorities. Like any man on parole, he is technically still liable for the balance of his sentence should he fall into trouble again. In practice, however, he is a free man. There is no surveillance and no parole board to report to. He can live anywhere in Cuba.

Lee Lockwood, *Castro's Cuba, Cuba's Fidel: An American Journalist's Inside Look at Today's Cuba.* New York: Macmillan, 1967.

there to help fill the vacancies? But the situation in Havana is not so perfect. How could it be? The history of the city is so different. Its organization is different. The opportunities are of a different order. And we have to remember that the Government has released more people on to the labour market, because our women have been helped with their very young children, so they too are looking for jobs. With their very young children in free day nurseries and the older children in boarding schools or on scholarships, the women have filled out the labour force. The family income is better, you see. And perhaps I should tell you that there has been, because of the Government's labour policy, an increase in the real wage of the worker nationally. I think it is roughly about seventy per cent, maybe a little less, but it was made possible because of the burdens I told you about, the burdens of high rents and so on, being lifted. We even have canteens in our factories where the food is free. And other free facilities and amenities for the workers. Something else: we've got work-and-wages departments in Cuba, and they watch over the balance that must be maintained in the industrial and agricultural sectors. So there has been a moderate increase in wages, yes. And the people aren't being ignored and taken for granted any longer, as they used to be. They're helped where it really matters. They're much better off now because of the radical changes in our way of looking at life in Cuba.

Social Security, Cuban Style

Salkey: What are the benefits from social security like?

Student: The Revolution changed the old laws straight away. First of all, I remember that in 1959 there was a decree that protected the victims of the people's struggles against Batista. Right after that, the Bank of Social Security was set up. It looked after all the institutions that had to do with the disabled, the old people, national insurance and so on. People who weren't covered were, after the opening of the Bank, some forty per cent of the people, from airline employees and night club entertainers to coffee plantation workers and salt miners, a whole wide range, including the rice and sugar workers and the tomato pickers, everybody. Retirement payments were fixed, and pensions, at about forty to forty-five pesos a month. In nearly ninety-five per cent of the cases, before the new laws, the retirement and pensions payments were well under thirty-eight pesos. Everybody's allotted payments were bumped up. That's the Bank of Social Security, you see. Of course, there's also the professional workers' scheme. And there's a complex system of keeping everything under the Ministry of Labour and the National Bank of Cuba. But Social Security works, now, in the interest of all the people.

Rehabilitating Political Prisoners

Salkey: May I change the topic radically for a moment?

Student: As you like.

Salkey: Fidel mentioned in 1965, I think, that there were some twenty thousand political prisoners in the country. What's the position here?

Student: Well, that is so. There are political prisoners and quite a lot of them. I don't know if your figure is right. But there are many in prison here. The Republic has external and internal enemies you know.

Salkey: I know that. But what's being done about the enormously long sentences, in some instances as long as twenty or thirty years, and so on?

Student: What can we do about other people's crimes against us but check them whenever and wherever we can, for the protection of the State? That's all we can do to safeguard the Revolution. Every country does that. We can't afford to be slack about a thing like sabotage or disloyalty or counter-revolution. We aren't unique in wanting to protect our people and their Government.

Salkey: Does it worry you, personally? The people? Fidel?

Student: It is worrying, yes. For all concerned. We are a free people. More than a quarter of a million Cubans have left Cuba since the Revolution, you know. We don't stop anybody from leaving. About a thousand a month still leave as they may and they go unmolested. They leave much behind, by law, but they're free to go. Yes, it is worrying to know that there are political prisoners in the country. We would like to have none at all. But what can we do?

Salkey: What's being done for them?

Student: Well, Fidel was a prisoner too, as you may remember. He knows about that sort of thing. He knows about the damage it can do to the spirit. And he is sympathetic and politically sensible about the matter. He has offered rehabilitation courses to many of the prisoners in Cuba. They can be re-educated to take their place in the new society, if they want. That is only right, I think.

Salkey: Do many say yes to re-education?

Student: Some do. And the scheme is working very well, as far as I know. I haven't any figures, but I do know that a lot is being done about re-education and rehabilitation.

Salkey: What is the ultimate aim of the re-education scheme?

Student: To allow them to re-enter the society when they show they're ready to do so. They may never show they're ready. It is risky, but it must be done, or attempted at least. We've got social justice now, and we live up to it, not just pay lip-service to it at Congresses. We fought hard for it, to set it up, and now that we've got it, we make use of it in the way we treat one another. It doesn't only harden the criminal or the political prisoner to leave him in prison for twenty or thirty years, it makes him rot and lose everything. Re-education is helpful all round and it is revolutionary. But we can't just empty the prisons of all the political prisoners and let them go in the same frame of mind as they went inside. What would happen doesn't bear thinking of, if it were possible. Our political prisoners—I don't think of them as a blot on the Revolution, as some foreigners do. If we catch people trying to destroy what we're building, what do we do? Allow them to do so again by letting them out without due care for the society? That doesn't make sense.

Salkey: It's still a problem?

Student: It is.

Getting Rid of Money

Salkey: And the other side? What're some of the new plans? The ones we've heard about quite recently, involving the possibility of a social revolution in the Revolution, if that's the right way of putting it?

Student: Debray[1] won't mind. [He laughs.] Well, Fidel is an idealist and a realist all at once, as everybody knows. This is good for a small country. Even for a large country, it's still essential. He wants to bring about a Utopian situation in one sector but he is cautious too.

Salkey: What sector?

Student: He would like, one day, to do away with private property ownership and money altogether. For instance, our Telegraph Company is still American, technically, with a Cuban manager, of course, to see that our interests are served, but it's privately owned, in a way. The telegraph service, with the laying of undersea cables, is an expensive business, so we keep the old arrangement going, in a sense. It suits us to. But back to what you asked. Fidel wants to get rid of money. He wants free housing, free transport, free theatres and movies, free shops, free everything you can think of for Cuba. He sees society without the exchange of money, the incentive of money, the bad history of money. He sees it with new people in it, people without the need of money. This is the dream he has. The new people won't work for the material rewards we all know, for the customary inducements, even in a Communist State; they will work for something else then, something more finally enriching and liberating, I suppose, really. The negative side will die. Money will die. The positive side will come into play. He envisages a man performing a task for reasons of honour, let's say, or maybe for a greater ideal than he has at present. Work will no longer be just a piece of material stuff, providing money and providing creature comforts; it will be a positive contribution towards establishing, with enormous will of course, a new and greater Communism.

1. Regis Debray, author of *Revolution in the Revolution?* (1967)

Salkey: Will it ever happen, d'you think?

Student: Our Revolution happened. Yes, I believe it will. Most of the young people will believe.

Salkey: The young will?

Student: Not only the young. It's more than mere enthusiasm. It takes faith. Faith in ourselves. The young and the not so young have faith. We have faith now. Fidel's Utopia will take extraordinary faith, extraordinary planning and very, very extraordinary hard work. That's all.

Chapter 3

Justice for All

Chapter Preface

The transition from a neocolonial economy to a Socialist economy required such a tremendous amount of effort that there never seemed to be enough people to do all the work. To this end, Socialists in general strove mightily to include everyone, regardless of race or gender, in the workforce. Castro demonstrated his understanding of the necessity for race and gender equality by including Afro-Cubans and women in his revolutionary army. Upon taking command of Cuba, he continued to work to include minorities and women in the important work of building socialism, and he was particularly interested in helping them attain positions of leadership in the party and the government.

As a result, the revolution brought about significant improvements in the lives of Afro-Cubans and women throughout Cuba. Educational and job opportunities were made available to them in unprecedented numbers, as well as improved access to better housing and health care. Despite Socialist theory and Castro's best intentions, however, racism and sexism persisted in postrevolutionary Cuba, even as they did in the United States in the wake of the civil rights and feminist movements.

The revolution also worked to ensure that all Cubans were equal before the law. In prerevolutionary Cuba justice was a commodity that could be bought and sold. The municipal police and the rural guard were primarily tools of the upper class and foreign corporations, and they treated members of the working class harshly, at times even brutally. Under Castro, the lower courts were put into the hands of the people, and they began to dispense justice tempered with mercy. Security forces were still to be obeyed, but for the first time ever they were required to treat civilians with respect.

Attending a People's Court

Ernesto Cardenal

Before the revolution, the Cuban judicial system was more
concerned with maintaining order than with dispensing justice. Policemen often beat youths who congregated on street
corners or in plazas on the theory that these youths were
gangs about to commit some sort of crime. Cubans who were
convicted of minor offenses such as disturbing the peace were
routinely sentenced to jail terms of as much as six months.

Much of this changed after the revolution. Public security
personnel were expected to treat their civilian "comrades"
politely and reasonably, while civilians were expected to obey
with respect. In addition, people's courts were established
wherein, for minor offenses, one was tried in one's own
neighborhood by one's neighbors. Judges were likewise
elected from the neighborhood and trained to dispense justice
in such a manner that furthered the aims of the revolution.

Ernesto Cardenal was a Nicaraguan poet who visited Cuba
in 1970 and 1971. While there he talked with Cubans from all
walks of life in order to understand better what the Cuban
revolution was actually achieving. In this excerpt, he
describes his visit to a people's court in Havana. As his report
makes clear, this court closely resembles the "TV courts" that
became popular in the United States several decades later.

I thought they no longer existed, if they ever had. We were
eating in the dining room of the National Hotel, when I

Ernesto Cardenal, *In Cuba*, translated by Donald D. Walsh. New York: New Directions Publishing Corporation, 1974. Copyright © 1974 by Ernesto Cardenal, Donald D. Walsh, and
New Directions Publishing Corporation. All rights reserved. Reproduced by permission.

heard some of the South American judges and their wives say that that night they were going to go to a People's Court, while others said that they were going to the movies. In my mind I saw a mass of people in a park judging a counter-revolutionary and all shouting in chorus: Shoot him! Shoot him! I was surprised that they existed and that no one had talked about them, and even more, that now there was a completely natural discussion about whether to go to them or to some other spectacle. I asked if it was certain that there were People's Courts, and one of the Cubans told me that there were lots of them, in many parts of the city. He added: "Don't miss seeing them. They are one of the finest things about our Revolution." I said to myself: I've got to see that, for my book; and I shall put down, honestly, everything that happens there, even though it's something horrible.

Failure to Stop

We went in a bus, after supper. The Court was out toward Miramar, I think. A big building with a little garden in front, and a big outside porch that was used as a waiting room. Almost all the seats were occupied, a big attendance, some children, little blacks who listened with great attention and giggled. On a platform the judges: a black lady with graying hair, a mulatto also with gray hair, a fat and very white lady. A young doctor, dressed in white, and an old mulatto militiaman were being questioned. The white lady was interrogating the doctor in a rather merciless way: "You're a doctor, aren't you?" "Yes, comrade." "And you are aware of the law that prohibits taking children on visits to hospitals?" "I was more or less aware of it." "And you heard the comrade militiaman tell you to stop your car because you couldn't take that girl to the hospital?" "He shouted at me very crudely, and I preferred not to argue with him and to keep going, because I had no intention of taking my daughter into the hospital. I was going to leave her outside in the car." "As we have made clear, from the guard post to the hospital it is scarcely three hundred yards. Couldn't you have left your daughter in the car at the guard post and gone to the hospital on foot?" "It didn't occur to me.

I only thought that I wasn't intending to take her into the hospital but to leave her in the car, and that the comrade militiaman had no reason to stop me."

And the questions went on: Didn't he know that a child was more apt to catch a virus than an adult since its tender organism has fewer defenses? Was it not evident that he, as the father of the child (and as a doctor besides), was more obliged than anyone else to protect the health of his child? And didn't he believe that in exposing a child to the danger of contracting an illness he was endangering the health of many other children in school who might come in contact with his daughter? And didn't he believe that a doctor should be the first person to respect a health law? And didn't the comrade militiaman order him to halt, reminding him that it was forbidden to take children visiting in hospitals? Doesn't every citizen have the obligation to obey a militiaman who is performing his duty?

The black gray-haired lady afterward questioned the militiaman: Did he speak to the doctor in an angry voice? The militiaman said he didn't, that he spoke politely, that perhaps he did raise his voice when he saw that he wasn't being obeyed. . . . Does he admit, then, that he got angry? He said yes, maybe he could have got angry. And doesn't he believe that it is wrong for a militiaman to speak to a civilian in a rude and ill-mannered way? He admitted that it was, and that on that count he might have acted badly, why should he deny it? (The doctor intervened to say that the man spoke to him very coarsely, or really that he was like a wild beast.) The white lady asked the militiaman if it was true that he had threatened. He said no: he had never told the doctor that he was going to shoot him, but that "he might have shot him." The lady said: "Well, I call that threatening. When a person says that with a weapon in his hand, that's threatening to kill. Or it could be understood that way."

The Jury's Decision

The judges retired to deliberate. The Argentine Walsh [one of the author's companions] said "That doctor is done for."

There is a little sign: NO SMOKING. This surprises me because it's an open area, practically a porch in front of a little courtyard. But it's even more surprising that the sign should be obeyed in a Latin country. In order to smoke we had to go into the courtyard. The jury came back in a half hour, and everyone stood up. There was an intensely expectant silence, and the black lady began to read the sentence. She began by saying that the jury had made the necessary investigations beforehand, as it always has to, and had established the fact that the doctor came from a poor family, and that he pursued his studies with great sacrifices before the Revolution, working at night and supporting his widowed mother, and that from the beginning of the Revolution he had shown himself a revolutionary, being at Girón Beach [the Cuban name for the Bay of Pigs, where Cubans repulsed a U.S.-backed invasion] and volunteering medical aid in Algeria, where he won high distinction, for which the jury congratulated him. Applause from the public. Afterward, it had established the fact that the militiaman was equally revolutionary, he had also fought at Girón Beach, he had been a Model Worker (porter in a plant), took part in many harvests, and that in spite of his sixty-five years of age and his infirmities, he continued to give voluntary services, taking his turn in military duty, etc., etc., and the jury congratulated him, too. More applause. The jury regretted deeply that two authentic revolutionaries had had a conflict of this kind, in which both were at fault (the one for not having obeyed as he should have, the other for having issued an order in an angry tone), even though the jury found in each one reasons that explained those faults and considered them extenuating circumstances: the doctor was driving fast and did not hear the order distinctly, the order was given angrily and even threateningly. On the other hand, the militiaman was tired after many hours on guard duty, he suffered from rheumatism and it had been raining all afternoon, and the fact that he was disobeyed exasperated him and he lost his self-control. The judges advised them, as good revolutionaries, to forget their differences and not to get involved again in painful incidents like this one, which had brought them here instead of letting them enjoy these hours in the relaxation of their respective homes. And finally they were urged to continue lending their valuable services to society and to the Revolution as they had done up to then. Enthusiastic applause.

Leniency Toward the Homeless

The next case was that of a blonde girl, plump, coarse, accused of having occupied an empty room in a building without any right to it. "Did you know that you were committing an illegal act when you occupied that room without having any authorization?" "I knew that it was illegal." "And can you tell us why you did it?" "Because I had no place to live." "What? You had no place to live? And where did you used to live?" "I lived in the street, I had no home." "You say that you lived in the street. Give us more details. For example, where did you sleep?" "Wherever night overtook me." "That's not very helpful. We want to know explicitly in what places you slept when night overtook you. The night before you illegally occupied that room, where had you slept?" "I slept in a car parked in the street. I already told you I slept wherever night overtook me."

More questions followed. Did she work? No, she was not working then; her husband worked. She had a husband? Yes, but they were separated, she thought he didn't love her any more. They had recently come to Havana. They were from Las Villas. She lived with her family, in the country, etc., etc. The jury went out to deliberate. I thought: They won't congratulate this one like the others; I don't want them to find her guilty, but if I were a judge I would have to do so.

They returned. Everyone stood up. They read the sentence. Not guilty. The jury did not find it a crime that she had entered a room that was not hers, because it was discovered that the room was not locked. "The accused did not break any lock on entering that room and consequently did not violate any law, although obviously she is obliged to vacate it now that the authorities have instructed her to do so." Although it absolved the accused, the jury nevertheless wished to make the following recommendation: that she return to her parents' house in Las Villas, in the country, which might be a modest house with possibly a palm-tree roof, but after all it was home, and there they lived happily, and there they had an assurance of work, productive farm work, which is what is most needed now in Cuba, instead of being needlessly here in Havana, helping to aggravate the housing problem, which was already acute. . . . But this was only a simple recommendation and not an order, and meanwhile, whatever decision she made, the jury would give her an urgent reference to the Institute of Urban Reform and the Housing Center so that this painful situation might be solved, etc., etc. Applause. Marta Lynch beside me applauded enthusiastically and said: "What learned people! I would not know how to judge that case!"

Dealing with a Home Wrecker

The next case made the children laugh. It was the suit of two women who continued to quarrel right in front of the Court. A married woman was accusing another woman, divorced, of taking her husband away from her. The divorced woman was a sensual brunette with straight hair hanging down over half her face. A lie—she said—the wife had found them kissing. The husband had tried to kiss her against her will, and she was fighting him off when the wife appeared. The divorced woman was in their house because she had come to borrow half a bottle of olive oil, and the husband had shown her into the kitchen pretending that the wife was there and had tried to attack her there, and she was struggling to break away from him. No, said the wife, she was letting herself be kissed, and she broke away from him only when the wife surprised them. The wife was very jealous of her husband, said the divorced woman, because he didn't love his wife and was unfaithful to her and made love to every woman including the divorced woman, but she had never let him in, as the whole neighborhood knew. And then there was the quarrel that they had had right in the building, at the door of a neighbor's apartment, where the wife had called the other a whore and they had pulled each other's hair and the neighbors had had to separate them. She was talking peacefully with this neighbor—said the divorced woman—when the other one called her a whore from the stairwell. I didn't call her a whore until we were pulling hair, said the wife. She had shouted at her from the stairs because these women were making fun of her. . . . Several neighbors gave their testimony, but it was contradictory, and the quarrel at the apartment door got more and more embroiled, and tempers were getting hot again, and "whore" was being hurled back and forth in front of the judges—which made the kids and the grown-ups laugh out loud: "Whore was what she called me. . . ." "I didn't call her whore, she rushed at me. . . ." (And the judges had to ring the bell several times because the women were about to come to blows again.)

When they went out to deliberate it was late at night, and we still had to wait at least half an hour to hear the verdict, but none of us wanted to leave. We were much interested in learning how they were going to solve that very complicated case. "Now surely we will have a verdict of guilty," said Marta Lynch [another friend of the author]. "That woman is a bitch [referring to the divorced one]." I thought to myself: That's the way it ought to be. But, suppose she is innocent and the wife is a jealous woman, as she says? If I had been a judge in this case I wouldn't have been able to solve anything: I give up as a judge.

Everyone standing. The fat white lady read the sentence this time. Not guilty for the married woman, guilty for the divorced woman. The penalty imposed on the latter is, in the first place, a warning. The lady stopped reading from the paper, took off her glasses and then, in a gentle voice, gave her the warning. She said that the jury did not judge her with respect to her private life, which according to the testimony of neighbors had always been respectable and spotless, and that it did not wish to cast the slightest doubt upon her honor, but that it considered her guilty of *imprudence*, because when a woman goes to borrow something from a neighbor and discovers that she isn't home, but that only the husband is at home, she should refrain from going in, to avoid the gossip of the neighbors and the suspicions of the wife. . . . And even more in the case of a divorced woman, she ought to be especially wary of this gossip, etc., etc. And the second request of the jury is to go back to school, for it had learned that she had completed only the third grade, so she was asked to report her monthly marks to the Court. Applause. And Marta Lynch said: "Incredible: they punish her by sending her to school."

The Cuban Court System

They told us that the People's Courts tried minor crimes that, in the police code before the Revolution, were called police crimes and were settled if guilty by a fine or up to six months in jail. The major crimes were judged in the Criminal Courts, and the political crimes (or "crimes against the Revolution") were also judged in a separate court. The penalties that the People's Courts impose are usually, we were told, a public warning or, in certain cases, "removal" (work on a farm), and, only in very extreme cases, prison. The judges of the People's Courts are elected by the people in assemblies in each neighborhood, and after election they are given a thirty-day law course. A minimum sixth-grade education is required, and they must do their judging in the place where they live. Their work is unpaid, they do it in their free hours, and it is completely voluntary. Many other Courts like this one, we were told, are held in many parts of Havana every Thursday night. Some Courts are held right in the street. These People's Courts, besides resolving the minor conflicts in the community, are very educational for the people, and the people attend them with pleasure, like a movie.

I told the poet Pablo Armando Fernández that I had gone to a People's Court, and he said: "They are marvelous. They are something Greek and Biblical: they seem to be the people of Athens gathered in the agora. And the judges have the wisdom of Solomon." Back in Nicaragua I read in *The Press* a news item from the A.P. [Associated Press wire service]: "President Allende has been harshly criticized by the opposition for having spoken of instituting People's Courts in Chile, and the press and the radio have said that this is the first step toward the beginning of a reign of terror like that of Red China or Castro's Cuba. It was especially recalled that in Cuba the function of these People's Courts was to send political enemies before the firing squad."

Improving the Lives of Minority Women

María Antonia Carrillo

Before the Cuban Revolution, Afro-Cuban women were afforded little respect and few opportunities. About the best an Afro-Cuban woman could hope for was a life as a domestic servant to a wealthy white family. One of the things the revolution changed was to open doors for minorities and peasant women, particularly in terms of receiving an education and then acquiring meaningful and rewarding employment.

Judy Maloof is a professor of Spanish at the University of New Mexico. In 1992 she traveled to Cuba to interview a diverse group of women to learn more about the continuity of women's political activism in Latin America. In this excerpt, she interviews María Antonia Carrillo of Havana. Carrillo served in the Mariana Grajales platoon during the Cuban Revolution and eventually became the director of an Afro-Cuban dance troupe. She relates how much the revolution has done for Afro-Cubans and women, and that much remains to be done to eliminate racism and sexism from the island.

I was born in 1939 in the province of Cienfuegos. Before the Revolution this province was called Las Villas. I don't know if I can even say I had a childhood. It wasn't much of a childhood. During the early years of my life everything was such a struggle. My family was very poor, and we were struggling to survive. There were so many ups and downs. My grandparents lived here in Havana. My father worked cutting sugarcane in season, and during the off season he would come to Havana and work with my grandfather at the Cuatro Caminos market. He worked very hard to earn enough money so we could at least subsist. My mother worked too, as a domestic servant. This is how my three brothers and sisters and I grew up, just barely getting by.

Heritage and Education

Since the time I was a young child I was drawn to the Afro-Cuban religion Santería and to the practice of spiritualism (*espiritismo*). I grew up surrounded by many people who practiced this religion of African origin and who believed in the *orishas*, or African gods. My mother had an altar at home devoted to the *orishas*, and she taught me a lot about this religion. At an early age I began attending ceremonies and dances, and I'm still involved in this practice today. I have my little altar with my saints. I'm also very interested in everything related to my Afro-Cuban heritage, all the so-called "folklore," our traditional dances and music, the art, handicrafts, and other forms of popular culture. When I was a little girl I learned Afro-Cuban dances and songs, with African rhythms and lyrics.

Since my family was so poor, I was able to attend school only through the sixth grade. I went to school in a small town that's so small I don't even know if you can call it a town. I lived near enough to walk there, barefoot, together with my siblings. This region was so destitute that most of the kids didn't have any shoes to wear to school. It wasn't until after the Revolution that I was able to continue my education. I completed my high school degree at one of the schools in Havana started by the Federation of Cuban Women. It was part of the FMC's project to incorporate peasant and poor women into the work force.

Fighting for the Revolution

In the region I came from everybody supported the Revolution. Many peasants and workers on small farms in the area rose up and fought in the armed struggle against [Cuban dictator Fulgencio] Batista. When I was still a teenager, I had a boyfriend who was a combatant. His name was José Chacón. He would send me letters, and I would go to see him and take messages for other fighters from friends and families who lived nearby. I became more and more committed to the Revolution without really understanding why. Perhaps it was love—I loved José, I loved life, and I loved the Revolution. I didn't really have much political awareness or fully comprehend what the war was all about, but I was becoming increasingly involved. By the time I was eighteen, José had died in combat. The military had searched our home twice, and they took the only pair of shoes I owned. This is the story about how I got involved in the Revolution.

I was one of the women who fought in the all-woman platoon called Mariana Grajales. It was a beautiful experience. We were all so united and so in love with the Revolution. There weren't any bad feelings of rivalry or jealousy among us. I had to learn how to use a weapon; I didn't think I would be able to, but I did. The sense of revolutionary fervor that enveloped us was so strong that fighting back seemed like the only thing to do. It was the only way to get rid of the tyrannical dictator who was torturing and murdering so many of our *compañeros*. The only thing we cared about was to keep moving forward and to keep fighting. We fought in a number of battles near the end of the Revolution, during the last months of 1958. I will always carry with me, in my heart, the memories of this experience, and of the celebration and joy of our victory!

Working for Equality

After the triumph of the Revolution I worked with the Federation of Cuban Women. One of our first tasks was to go out into the countryside and try to persuade peasant women to come to the new schools established to teach them how to read and write. It wasn't easy, but I remember doing this work with such enthusiasm. It was a very difficult period for us because of the counterrevolutionaries, but I recall doing all of this work with a lot of love.

For me, personally, as a black woman in Cuba, the Revolution brought opportunities that I'd never even dreamed were possible. In prerevolutionary Cuba the only option for a black woman was to work as a domestic servant in the home of some wealthy white woman who lived in Miramar or some other fancy neighborhood, or maybe get a job as a waitress at a third- or fourth- or fifth-class joint. Most of the first-class restaurants and nightclubs preferred to hire white women. Because of racial discrimination in this country, very few blacks were able to get a university education before the Revolution. Even in my small town the whites strolled in the center of the park and expected us to stay on the edges—that is actually outside the park. I think racism was one of the main reasons why so many of us black Cubans joined the revolutionary forces. The rebels were fighting for a new society based on racial equality and on the equality of women.

In my opinion, there still isn't full racial equality in Cuba, but I don't think it's the fault of the government that there are so few black leaders in high positions of power. I am a militant in the PCC and our platform is one of racial and gender equality, but it's difficult to change racist attitudes that have existed for many generations. We still have a long way to go. Even Fidel asked in one of his speeches, "What has happened here? Why are there so few blacks and women elected to high-level Party positions?" I think the commander in chief was asking, "Why do racism and sexism still exist in Cuba?"

Government Support of Cultural Arts

So let me tell you, because of this new revolutionary government, I was able to get an education and to become who I am today. I am now directing an Afro-Cuban dance troupe. We just got back from a tour of Mexico! Do you think I could have even dreamed about traveling to Mexico before the Revolution? Or showing my paintings at art exhibitions? No way! I could never even have finished high school if it hadn't been for the new government. I think that the problems of racial discrimination and machismo still haven't been eradicated in the popular, grassroots sectors of Cuban society, but I don't think it's the government's fault.

I've been directing an Afro-Cuban dance troupe since 1985. It is very rewarding work. I love working with young people and teaching them about their heritage through dance. The government has been very supportive of the promotion of Afro-Cuban dance, music, and popular culture, which are seen primarily as part of our national folklore, not as related to any religious cult. Our dance troupe has performed at many hotels and convention and tourist centers, in addition to national festivals of popular culture. As I said, we were invited to Mexico City. I'm hoping we will be invited on another international tour.

Gender Equality

As for gender equality, I've had a happy marriage that has lasted more than twenty years, something that is rare today in Cuba. My husband, Oscar, is also black. He was a combatant in the clandestine movement, and since the triumph of the Revolution he has always had important leadership roles in areas related to the militias and to the defense of the Revolution. Because of all his responsibility, Oscar never spent much time at home. He would leave early in the morning and usually come home late at night; he often had to attend Party meetings in the evenings. But now that he is retired, we spend a lot more time together. My partner is very good about helping out at home. Actually, we get along very well regarding the running of the house. He is understanding, and if he has to go shopping for food, he goes. Oscar does most of the cooking, since he gets home before I do. He washes the dishes and helps out with most of the domestic chores.

In addition to my dance troupe activities, I paint. I began painting sometime around 1976, when I was already middle-aged, in my forties. I had my first exhibition in 1980, and I recently showed some of my work in Mexico City. I had the honor of participating in the Association of Cuban Artists and Artisans when it was first organized. Many important Cuban artists belonged to this group, William Sotomayor and others. I've always felt inspired to paint Afro-Cuban folk themes, mostly, *orisha* motifs, although some of my early work is landscapes. I paint with both acrylics and watercolors.

Increased Tolerance

As well as the strides made towards racial and sexual equality, recently there has been more tolerance and acceptance of all types of religious expression here in Cuba. Freedom of religion was discussed a lot at the last Party Congress. Not only *espiritistas* but people from many different religions are now allowed to worship openly. Before, it wasn't like they would put you in prison or break into your home to see if you were praying, but there was little tolerance of religion, of any religion. All good Marxists were supposed to be atheists. Fortunately, those attitudes and government policies have changed. Now it is possible to be a Party militant *and* openly express one's religious beliefs.

Now that there is more freedom of religious expression, an increasing number of young people have been initiated into Santería. And since they no longer fear losing their jobs or facing other hassles because of their religion, you can see people on the streets wearing colored, beaded necklaces that correspond to their particular saint. Until recently, most people practiced their religion at home, secretly, and would never discuss their beliefs openly. But this is changing. I believe, just as my African ancestors believed, that the gods are everywhere—in nature, in the air, in the trees, in the sun, and in the moon. Human beings may disappear, but the universe is everlasting. For me, this is my religion; this is my idea of God, and this is everything to me!

No Turning Back

I also want to tell you that if the gringos invade our island, I, María Antonia Carrillo, will be among the first to take up arms and fight in the trenches. There is no way I want to return to the prerevolutionary Cuba of misery and racial discrimination. I will die fighting for the ideals of our Revolution before submitting to a return to Yankee imperialism on the island. Sure, we have serious problems. It would be a lie not to admit that we have problems. There are shortages of lard and cooking oil and lots of things. But we need to be able to endure and to resist. Nobody is dying of hunger in Cuba. Our soil is fertile, and it gives us fruits and vegetables, and we have sugar. So we can survive. As you know, if you get sick or need an operation, it is free. You don't have to pay anything. Of course, I hate our policy of tourism, just as a lot of Cubans hate it. I don't think it's fair that everything in Cuba is for the tourists and nothing is for us, the Cubans. I can still be a revolutionary and not like everything about my country. But I do think the Cuban people are very creative, and we need to come together to find solutions to our problems. This is the only way we can survive this economic crisis, and the only way the Revolution can survive.

Combating Racial Discrimination

Elpidio de la Trinidad Molina, Jorge Molina,
and Egipcia Perez

In addition to fighting sexism, the revolution also sought to do away with racism, and for the same reasons. Racism is incompatible with basic socialist ideals, and there was too much work to be done to deny anyone the opportunity to do some of it simply because of the color of their skin. To this end, the revolution made education more accessible to Afro-Cubans, and encouraged them to get involved in revolutionary groups in order to build socialism on the island.

In practice, racial equality was no easier to achieve than gender equality. Although Afro-Cubans made real strides as a result of the revolution, racial stereotypes that had prevailed for years before the revolution refused to die. When Cuba began to promote tourism and entrepreneurialism during the Special Period, the aftermath of the collapse of communism in Europe, racism returned with renewed vigor.

Pedro Pérez Sarduy and Jean Stubbs are scholars who focus on Caribbean and Latin American studies. Between 1995 and 1997 they interviewed a number of Afro-Cuban professionals to find out how the revolution had affected their lives; this excerpt presents three of those interviews. In the first, Elpidio de la Trinidad Molina declares that the revolution changed his life profoundly and for the better. In the second, his son, Jorge Molina, concurs to a certain degree, but acknowledges that racism still persists in Cuba. In the third, Egipcia Perez presents a harsher view of Cuban racism, one that suggests that, in some cases, the Revolution made only a tiny dent in the racist attitudes of white Cubans.

Elpidio de la Trinidad Molina

I was born on 27 May 1923 in Havana. I am married and have five children. My father was a barber and my mother a seamstress. We went through hell during the dictatorship of Gerardo Machado. To survive, we boys had to clean porches, sometimes a whole house, and we'd carry buckets of water for just a few cents a day to help out the family. Things were very cheap, but it was real hard even to put together a few cents. There were six of us, three boys and three girls. I was the second oldest. During that whole period we lived in slums, in a tiny room where the family could barely fit. Only my mother really knew what we were going through, trying to make ends meet to pay for the room at two pesos a month. We lived in fear of being evicted—that they'd throw our furniture out on the street and we'd have to find someplace else to live. Those days a haircut cost five cents for children, eight or ten cents for grown men, when they had it cut, because there wasn't the money for it, not even five or ten cents . . . it was a luxury. You'd get a haircut for your birthday, or May 20, Independence Day, or October 10, another patriotic day, or for *Noche Buena* [Christmas Eve], but our Christmas Eve was pretty sparse. We couldn't celebrate with pork, only pig's offal. After the Day of the Kings, a long time after January 6, maybe two or three months passed before my mother would have the money to buy each of us a spinning top or yo-yo, or a rag doll for the girls. But my mother did manage to find a way to send us to school and all six of us, first the boys and then the girls, finished primary school through sixth grade. I was able to go on through seventh and eighth grades, passed the entrance exam for the Havana Higher School for the Trades, and there I graduated as a chemical analyst and an industrial chemist. When I was eighteen, back in 1941–42, I was fortunate to start work where I still am today. I worked days and studied nights, to teach industrial chemistry, which is what I wanted.

Racism in the 1940s

We knew that because of the color of our skin we had to study hard, because through studying we would have more of a chance of getting a job. It wasn't easy. The worst jobs were for us blacks—a bricklayer's mate, because it wasn't even easy to become a bricklayer.

Way back, when I started primary school, I'd roller-skate all the way from Mantilla to Diez de Octubre, in Lawton, and back. I started to study for my baccalaureate, but that wasn't going to give me a trade. At the university, for example, the technical courses were for civil engineering and architecture. I wanted to do chemistry, and there wasn't chemical engineering, only agricultural engineering. I knew that I'd never find a job as an agricultural engineer. They were needed for the two or three soap factories there were at the time and they didn't employ blacks. I couldn't have worked in agriculture either, because the large estates were also for whites. In applied chemical engineering in the sugar industry, I wouldn't have found a job in a sugarmill. So I decided to go to trade school and graduated as an industrial chemist.

In the midst of all that, the Second World War started and some German Jews opened an emery stone factory. They moved into a house that belonged to the Alfonso family, who knew my mother, and the Germans asked if they knew of a young man who could help them. The family recommended me and I had the great luck to learn the trade. Now I'm an emery stone expert. I had the great luck of being helped at a certain stage in my life by whites who had quite a lot of power. I owe it to them for part of my education and well-being. In that sense, I can say I've been a privileged black.

The Revolution Opened Doors for Black Men

The knowledge I had I gave to the revolution. When the owners went to the United States, I was left in charge of the factory with one of the sons who didn't know much about production. The son stayed and I was the technical person, because I had already graduated from trade school. When the revolution opened up the universities, I did a year's training and then studied what I'd always wanted to study and hadn't been able to, chemical engineering. But then after two years I switched to a degree in chemistry. I didn't graduate in either, but I did acquire the knowledge I could later apply in emery stone production. It also stood me in my stead when [minister of industries] Comandante Che [Guevara] visited our factory. By then he'd already said, "Worker, build your own machinery," and we were building ours. Putting together the information and with his inspiration, we developed a whole emery stone technology for the many varieties that are used in a country's development. That helped us hold out against the imperialist blockade that started after 1 January 1959. I remember when Fidel arrived here on 8 January 1959, he said in his first speech that blacks had been given the coral rock, because we couldn't visit the sandy beaches, only a bit at Guanabo. For us blacks there was Santa Fe Beach, and Biriato, which closed under capitalism; we were left with only Jaimanitas and Santa Fe beaches, which were full of sea urchins and coral rock. Today we can go to all the beaches the magnates would go to, from one end of the island to the other, without discrimination.

Awards and Innovations

For all that I've done for the revolution I've received numerous awards, right from the start. In 1962, I was National Vanguard of the Silicate Enterprise, which covered cement, tile, and brick for furnaces and house construction. In 1963 I was also National Vanguard. Between 1959 and 1963 I made some twenty or thirty innovations. In 1962 I was chosen as a founding member of the Socialist Revolution United Party (PURS). In 1965 it was named the Communist Party of Cuba. Up until today, I've been a member. For the merits I've been given, from 1976 to 1994 I have been National Vanguard of the Construction Workers Union. I've also been

Provincial and National Vanguard of ANIR (the National Association of Innovators and Rationalizers). I have many medals and diplomas, and the highest recognition that can be given to any worker, which is that of Hero of Labor of the Republic of Cuba, since 1990. This recognition has only been given since 1985–86. There are fewer than one hundred workers in the whole of Cuba who have it. . . .

In the early days, as innovators we didn't receive any economic remuneration, only moral incentives. That changed later. After 1980, some workers received between 500 and 1,500 pesos for an invention. That was one incentive Fidel wanted to give us, because we'd received other incentives over the years; we'd been given beach houses to stay in, at Varadero and Guanabo. I've also had the honor of being on the 26 July Tribune, with Fidel. I've taken part in congresses of the party, the CTC (Confederation of Cuban Trade Unions), ANIR, and all that. Today, aged seventy-two, I calculate I must have made more than 150 innovations. . . .

Today I'm happy to see there are as many blacks in science and engineering as there are in medicine. This is undeniably due to the revolution. There is no discrimination, either by gender or race; 52 percent of professionals are black. Among the women, there are black and white women, as there are black and white men. There is no discrimination. That problem's behind us. The revolution fought it. This is a real revolution.

Jorge Molina

There are times when I sit and meditate on all the possibilities we blacks had at the start of the revolution to study at the university and even abroad. I studied chemical engineering, specializing in tiles and refractory materials, at the leading Moscow Mendiev Institute. There was a whole explosion of students who were able to choose their study. Of the five of us in my family, four boys and one girl, there was no push that we all be engineers. The opportunity was there. I'm the second of the family. The oldest, my sister, chose another subject at the university, because she wanted to earn a qualification, not because she was interested in the subject. She dropped out and started work but then combined work and study to get an economics degree. The brother after me studied electronics to work as a middle-level electrician. He has always found work. The next youngest, right from primary school, wanted to go into the military. He was sure of what he wanted, though he isn't someone who expressed himself easily. We're a respectful and united family, a product of how we were brought up in the home. Though black, we grew up in a neighborhood where practically the only black family was ours. From the start, we had to adjust to that life; we were able to live in a comfortable house because my mother was also a professional, in pharmaceuticals. That placed us in the Havana black middle class.

The Persistence of Racism

I remember a story my father once told me when I was little. He was studying and already had a good salary. One day a white told him to his face, "I may be a shoemaker, but I'm better than you, even though you've studied, simply because you're black." That still holds. Recently there's been a resurgence [of racism] because not only can certain businessmen in the new joint ventures choose their personnel for their skills, they can eliminate persons of the black race. The tourism which is coming in may have certain requirements and you simply find they don't accept blacks, even when the black may be educated, speak several languages, and have training in accountancy. You can't help see it. It's there. Cubans confuse ethnicity and nationality. You see that a lot when you go abroad. I studied in the former Soviet Union. There, we would be asked our racial origin, and we didn't know what to reply, whether Bantú, Yoruba, or Carabalí. They didn't know why we didn't know, because the white Cubans, of a different racial origin, said they were Cuban.

Today those managers simply don't want blacks among their workers. They identify with you as Cuban, which is what we are, but, whether a joint or Cuban venture, management doesn't want blacks. I know of an experience of a friend of mine. One day he heard he had been promoted to a company where he would be in charge of a tourist taxi firm which had some stringent requirements. The drivers had to speak at least three languages, be 1 m, 85 cm tall . . . I added, "and preferably white." He said, "Not preferably— they had to be white." And that's happening in many areas. It's the reverse of what was applied some years back with blacks, youth, and women. In part, I'm the product of that policy in the second half of the 1980s. It became a campaign to include blacks. I was called on to administer my workplace when I was a technician because the administrator had been promoted, not only because I knew languages and the technology of the factory, but also because I was young and black. But all that was ephemeral and came to an end, and as blacks we were left to head the unions and work in construction. There are very few of us who are enterprise managers. But I was also elected to a provincial government organization—as an innovator, which was something passed on to me by my father—where the provincial administrative posts are not exactly in black hands. Yet I'm indignant when I come across a person of the black race speaking against the revolution, because I'm convinced that blacks never lived better before the revolution. My parents taught me that. . . .

Egipcia Perez

I was born in Surgidero de Batabanó, in the south of Havana province. My childhood was pretty hard because I lost my mother when I was very little and was brought up by my grandmother on my mother's side. My two aunts looked after me and my sister, respectively. Though I didn't know much about life, I thought everything was fine, at seven I had already had to work. My father was a fisherman and, after being at sea for two or three months, there'd be times when he'd try to make seven to ten pesos after selling the owner's catch. Sometimes he'd only make three. The fishermen had to deduct their costs—fuel, food, and other supplies. What was left was divided among them. The fishermen were poor whites and blacks of the region, while the boat owners and dealers were always white.

My aunt was a home dressmaker and when I was nine she sat me at a sewing machine to make my first dress. It was to celebrate Fisherman's Day. My aunt said I could make myself a dress if I wanted. The whites had their Lyceum Sports Club and the Spanish Casino, but no black or mulatto, or anyone with any black in them at all, could go into either of them. We blacks had the Progress Society, an old, run-down place where the sponges were cut and kept, that would be fixed up for our festivities. That's when I made my first dress.

"You Don't Seem Black"

I went to school, but since I was always ambitious and, it would seem, clever, when I was nine I was already in junior high. The director, who was white and comfortably off, and called Pelayo Suárez Orta, said in admiration one day, "Egipcia, you really study, you don't seem black." According to him, I didn't have the backward ideas of other blacks for whom it was all the same to sew or clean . . . he saw another spirit in me. He asked why I didn't go on to study. When I told my father, he said I was crazy, where was the money going to come from. I argued I would sew and with the money from my sewing I'd pay for my studies. When I told my aunt who was bringing me up and who I called Mima, she said she'd help. She was the dressmaker, and I'd do the hemming. She'd pay me twelve to twenty cents a dress, and that way I put together the money to study at Doctor Pelayo Suárez Orta's academy. . . .

Time passed and I finished eighth grade and went to an academy here in Havana, in Cerro, because there was nothing in Batabanó to prepare me for going on to teacher training. I was around fourteen. I had no rest: from work to school, from school to the academy, from the academy to work, and on it went. Those who went to that academy stood a good chance of getting into the teacher training school or the home economics school, one or the other. I did the exam and didn't get in because I was black. . . . So I went to the home economics school, which was much further away and which I didn't like at all. That's when my studies came to an end. I didn't continue and went to work as a maid.

My first job was in the home of the director of my school in Batabanó, who was living close by in my neighborhood. She was called Haydée. I think her husband was also a minister. We had by then moved to Havana. That town was too poor to live in, much less to get on. So I became the nanny of a lovely little boy we called Pituco. It seems Haydée and the others in the house liked the fact that I was such a refined black woman. But the boy wanted to be carried always, and, since I was black, it was my duty to carry him so everyone would know I was the maid—in crisp white uniform. In those days, we would go on the weekend to Tarará beach, which was for whites, not blacks. I could go in because of what I was. But Haydée didn't want me always to be carrying the boy. I gradually got the boy used to the pram, or the playpen, or holding my hand, and gently taught him to speak. Haydée's husband would watch and say, "She doesn't seem black!" Always the same thing.

Haydée asked me why I had such long nails and beautiful hands. Her husband replied for me: "Because she's decent, because it looks good." Her response was, "Well, you must cut them." She didn't look after her own nails. I had to do everything for that boy, from washing his clothes to preparing his food. And people who visited the house would comment on my dress and my hands while I also looked after the boy. She hated this so much that she dismissed me one day. . . .

The Revolution Opened Doors for Black Women

At the time of the revolution, I had three children and took on two new zone organizations—the Committee for the Defense of the Revolution and the Federation of Cuban Women. Into my hands came forms to be filled out by persons wanting future work. I started work in the pharmacy that was next door to my house as a sector person: my job was to report to a doctor at Lawton Polyclinic. I would write out the prescriptions and she was surprised I had such good writing and spelling. Since it was close to home, I'd go and see to the children and then go back to work. Then a course came along which interested me a lot and I became a pharmaceutical technician, and that's what I did for twenty-nine years, until I retired.

In this second stage of my life I started work as an auxiliary at Julio Trigo Hospital. There I really came up against people because my ideas were not those "of blacks." When I didn't understand how things could be a certain way, I would say so, and the directors didn't like how I would stand out above the rest. But it was simply that I felt compelled to say what I didn't understand. I had a colleague there who would say, "Never protest, because when you do it'll cost you your job." But since I didn't work to eat but because I liked my work and wanted to be independent, I went on protesting if things were not right. I reasoned that if I were dismissed I would work somewhere else. . . .

Persecution

Later on I went to work at the worst pharmacy in the Víbora, one with a large personnel. I was the only black woman in my department and right from the start I crossed paths with a woman doctor who was like a whip. Customers would ask for me, not her, saying I treated them differently. The other two in charge took her side and would comment on money and medicines that were missing, saying the employees were to blame. Coincidentally, the employees were black. One day I told one of them that it wasn't the employees who were taking things: "The ones who rob here are the intelligent ones, you whites!" I was taken to a work council on charges of lack of respect. But they had to hear me out, because there I spoke about how I saw them taking medicines for their friends.

The persecution was so frequent and hostile that, in one

of those cases, a lawyer told me that if I had so much as taken a single aspirin I'd go to jail. It wasn't against me as a person but as the *negra* (black woman), to say, "The black woman took such and such." But there were whites who robbed constantly and were never caught. The sad thing is that not all blacks confront these racist attitudes. That's why I finally decided to retire.

Chapter 4

Surviving Without Soviet Aid

Chapter Preface

B ecause of the U.S. trade embargo, Cuba's most important trading partners were the Communist nations of Eastern Europe. When communism began collapsing in those countries in 1989, Cuba lost the bulk of its export market and had to look for income-making opportunities elsewhere. The post-1989 years became known as the Special Period in Cuba, a time of economic hardship during peace.

One economic reform Castro allowed, albeit reluctantly, was to encourage foreign visitors to come to Cuba, as they had in prerevolutionary days. The government built a number of tourist-only hotels and restaurants and restricted Cuba's finest beaches for their private use. A number of dollars-only stores were opened that carried top-quality merchandise at reasonable prices, all designed to separate tourists from even more of their money.

The influx of tourists also led to the return of small businesses in Cuba. Although the major means of production remained firmly in government hands, enterprising Cubans were permitted to open small restaurants, operate private taxicabs, and sell art and handcrafts on the streets. Others turned into *jineteros*, young men who sold black-market goods or served as tour guides, and *jineteras*, young women who provided "companionship" to the tourist trade. Despite these opportunities to make extra cash, many young people became disillusioned with Cuban socialism and longed to escape what they perceived to be a life without opportunity in their native land. At the same time, older Cubans who remembered what life had been like before the revolution took a different view of the Special Period—that despite its deprivations things had been worse during prerevolutionary times.

A Taste of How Most Cubans Live

Carlo Gebler

The decline of Soviet communism in the 1980s meant the end
of Soviet subsidies for the Cuban economy. To help replace
the subsidies, Castro opened Cuba's doors to foreign tourists.
Swanky hotels and restaurants were constructed for their
exclusive use. Tourist-only stores, where pesos were not
accepted, were stocked with high-quality, reasonably priced
merchandise. Meanwhile, the Cuban masses were forced to
shop and dine at second-rate establishments that offered
lower-quality goods and provided indifferent service.

Carlo Gebler was an English author who had become fas-
cinated with Cuba as a youth. In 1987 he, his wife, and their
daughter spent three months driving from one end of Cuba to
the other. In this excerpt, they exchange dollars for pesos with
black-market money changers in Havana. Then they dine at a
pizzeria and ice cream shop that cater to locals in order to get
a better idea of how the average Cuban lives.

The day after the beach we had lunch with Marge. She
was a US citizen who'd lived in Cuba since the early
Sixties. We were sitting in the Sierra Maestra, the restaurant
at the top of what used to be called the Havana Hilton and
is now called—a lovely little revolutionary sarcasm this—
the Havana Libre. At the next table two newlyweds were
eating baked Alaska.

We were talking about the Cuban economic system in
comparison to that in the West.

'Under capitalism,' said Marge, 'the worker is insecure about his job but once he's earnt his money, he can buy whatever he wants, provided he's earnt enough. In Cuba it's the reverse. Everyone, more or less, has a job and everyone has some money. The worker's anxiety instead is channelled into consumption, into getting hold of scarce goods.'

Luxury Stores

One focus, perhaps *the* focus of Cuban consumer desire, is the Dollar and Tecno shops which are all over the country. There was a whole complex of them on the ground floor of the Havana Libre which we had already explored. In these air-conditioned emporia, in absolute contrast to the shops on the streets, there were Japanese refrigerators and fans and jewellery and cosmetics, US cigarettes and Coca-Cola and all sorts of other luxury goods. There was an abundance of them, they were reasonably priced and they were of high quality; and this was only a small selection, we gathered, compared to what some of the mammoth Tecno stores had on offer. But such shops were for foreigners only, tourists or technicians with hard currency.

Despite socialism, however, the Cuban people have remained the sons and daughters of Adam. Years of indoctrination have eliminated neither the desire for goods nor the willingness to resort to devious means to obtain them. There is an enormous currency black market in Cuba, far bigger than anything I'd experienced when I had travelled in Eastern Europe. At the time of our conversation with Marge, we'd already had in the previous two days some twenty approaches in the street to change money. It was obviously a world we were going to have to penetrate. It happened two days later, without its being planned.

The Desire for Dollars

It was late morning. We were under a covered walkway at the bottom of the Paseo de Martí, just on the edge of Old Havana and half a dozen blocks away from the Museum of the Revolution. We could dimly hear the amplified roll call that played there continuously over the public address system. There were shuttered shops and men leaning against dirty, ragged pillars, spitting, smoking, picking their teeth, a battered 1957 Buick Century Riviera parked by the kerb and a strong smell of cat. A youth stepped in front of us. He was thin and black with curly hair and couldn't have been more than eighteen years old.

'Five to one, five to one . . .' he sang, shifting nervously from one leg to the other and looking furtively around. We both made a pretence of thinking seriously about his offer while India [the author's daughter] skipped about on the pavement. We didn't want to get arrested and deported. In the event, there were no police to be seen, only the men we'd already passed under the arches. I agreed. We would change twenty dollars. He would give us one hundred pesos.

A second youth loomed up behind the other, undid the zip pocket of his parachute trousers and pulled out a dirty roll of Cuban pesos.

I started to count. They didn't look like the pre-revolutionary notes which we'd been warned against. I got as far as twenty-five and stopped. I realised I was frightened. I looked up and all the faces along the arcade seemed to be staring at us in an unfriendly way.

'Police,' hissed the first youth.

Sod it, I thought. The twenty-dollar bill vanished from my hand and they were gone. We hurried across the road away from the staring faces and counted properly. We'd been duped. We'd got two pesos to the dollar.

A few minutes later in a smaller side street, we fared better. A solitary youth, a mulatto with an unshaven face, came up and asked if we wanted to change. I remembered his face from the arcade and I realised they had probably all been money-changers and their looks had not been malevolent but envious.

We agreed. He went over to a man standing in a crumbling doorway. The man was middle-aged and wore a cream suit and a straw hat and had a straggly moustache. He gave the youth a roll of money for us inside a copy of the national newspaper, *Granma*. I counted the pesos while pretending to read an item, put the dollars in the paper, rolled it up and gave it back to the youth. He said goodbye. We went on our way.

What happened to our dollars, I imagine, was as follows. The man with the moustache used them to buy items from Tecno or Dollar shops. (How the Cubans, who were banned from such establishments, got in to make their purchases was another story.) These items were then sold on the black market at vastly inflated prices. The pesos so obtained were then used to buy further dollars at an extraordinary exchange rate of five, six, seven to one. Sales of items on the black market would also provide the money-changer with an income to live on.

Do as the Cubans

Now we had pesos, we decided it was time to enter the Cuban mainstream. No more the Sierra Maestra at the top of the Havana Libre. We were going to do as the Cubans.

We had noticed the Pizzeria Milan in Vedado. We retraced our steps there. Its entrance was obscured by an enormously long queue which was not for the pizzeria but for an ice-cream stall twenty-five yards down the street.

We went through the queue and into the Milan and found ourselves in a long, gloomy room. Stretching down the whole length was a counter which curved like a roller-coaster track with about fifty fixed stools in front of it. Every seat was occupied and there was someone waiting behind almost every one of them. Along the side wall, there was another queue of about 200 people for the take-away counter at the back. Add to these the queue of ice-cream *aficionados* we had had to get through in order to get inside, and the impression I had was that I was in the middle of a Babel of queues.

We each found a space behind a stool. I was behind a woman with curly hair. Her armpits were shaved so bare they seemed polished. The neon strips overhead, most of which were blown, began to swing gently in the faint breeze blowing from outside.

After perhaps half an hour (I don't know exactly how long, I was so bored I'd stopped looking at my watch), the customers at the little section of roller-coaster in front of us paid and left in unison, and we, along with the next wave, moved forward—about fifteen of us—to take their place.

The counterhand was middle-aged and portly. He cleared away, put a leaf of flimsy carbon between the first two leaves of a little book and started to take orders. Glancing over my shoulder, I saw that the next wave who would take our place were already waiting, and there was another wave waiting behind them again. It was lunchtime.

When he got to the third customer, the counterhand got his top copies and his duplicates out of order. He said, 'Tut-tut!' out loud and waggled his pencil in the air and shook his head as he leafed back to make the necessary alterations. The tut-tutting and the pencil wagging continued all the way along the line.

Finally, the counterhand got to us. To eat or drink there was either unlabelled Cuban beer called Claro, literally 'Clear', or Refresco, a sweet sickly orange drink, which I suppose was Cuba's answer to Fanta. To eat there was a straight choice as well: pizza with tomato or spaghetti with tomato. Following the lead of other customers, we ordered our drinks in duplicate.

A Taste of Reality

The spaghetti arrived in a soup plate, grey, thick and over-cooked, with sweating beads of cheese and a tomato paste which tasted of vinegar. Five minutes later came the pizza. The dough was thick and had a sour taste, and the topping of cheese and tomato tasted the same as that on the spaghetti, only it was hot and melted, rather than cold and separated.

Both dishes were disgusting. Of the fifteen people on our section of counter, not one finished their meal. This was the first fruit of our black-market transactions. The rest of the journey saw many more little ironies like this one.

We paid, and moved off. Outside the Milan stood a bent old woman with a handbag, wearing a starched dress, her face covered with white pancake, as women wore their make-up in the 1930s. I looked at her carefully, wondering if she was a remnant of the vanished bourgeoisie.

Now we joined the line for ice-cream. Many of those ahead of us took their scoops away in empty Coca-Cola cans with the tops cut off. After half an hour it was finally our turn. The vendor, a lady in blue slacks, very fat, was amazed we only wanted one cornet.

We walked up N Street in the direction of the hotel. The wind was blowing furiously, and schoolgirls were holding their tiny mustard-coloured skirts against their thighs. A gigantic cardboard box rattled down from the direction of the Hotel Capri and across our path. Tiny pieces of grit lifted by the wind stung the face, and pedestrians had their eyes screwed up.

The Lights Go Out

We reached the Colina just as it began to spot with rain. On our floor, we found all the shutters had been secured in anticipation of the coming storm. It came, and we lay on our beds looking through the window at the black sky and the silvery needles of rain sheeting down, and listening to the buses sloshing along the street below.

Suddenly, there was a tremendous explosion, so violent the glass rattled in the panes, and then another, even louder. It was the electricity sub-station across the road blowing. Naturally all the lights in the bedroom, and all over the district, immediately went out.

We lay until night fell, when the janitor brought us candles. The wax was like poor-quality glass with bubbles in it and the wick was like poor-quality yarn. The flame was yellow and died with the slightest breeze. Lying on the damp pillow I remembered the narrator in *Inconsolable Memories*[1] thinking the worst punishment he could be given would be to have to list everything, from combs to automobiles, from buttons to paint, which Cuba was going to have to buy from the Communist bloc because the US had slammed the door.

---

1. *Inconsolable Memories*, by Edmund Desnoes, is a novel about Cuba that the author had read as a youth. It sparked his interest in seeing Cuba firsthand.

From Black Marketeers to Entrepreneurs

C. Peter Ripley

In 1993 the Cuban government began allowing Cubans to establish their own small businesses. It also made it legal for Cubans to possess foreign currencies, including dollars, thus making it easier for them to sell goods and services to tourists who were now coming to Cuba in unprecedented numbers. Within a year, more than fifty thousand Cubans had received business licenses and were engaging in entrepreneurial activity, many in connection with tourism.

C. Peter Ripley was an American journalist who traveled frequently to Cuba. In this excerpt, he describes a visit to Havana in December 1994. Ripley is surprised to discover that many people who were once considered to be black marketeers are now allowed to do business openly. Although he notes with approval that a certain air of prosperity seems to have returned to Havana, he also acknowledges with some sadness that entrepreneurialism seems to be making Cubans more anxious and aggressive.

It was mostly bad news and refugees that came out of Fidel's island during the two years it took me to get back there. Rumors circulated in Miami about a spectacular increase in the number of rafters, about idle children of the Revolution smashing windows in Havana's tourist hotels, about power blackouts lasting as long as twelve hours a day, about a malnourished citizenry eating cats, about Castro facing his final hours. Such pessimistic stories and dismal predictions left me anxious about Cuba and the fate of my friends there. Cuba never let me feel indifferent.

Finally in December 1994 I flew to Nassau and caught an uneventful shuttle to Havana. Hailing a cab at José Martí Airport for the ride across Havana to the Hotel Inglaterra, I braced myself for the worst, certain I was about to enter a desperate and desolate place. But as was so often the case, Cuba was not what she was supposed to be. *Los amarillos*[1] were disappearing from the roads along with the crowds of hitchhikers, many of whom were riding buses donated by sympathetic cities in Canada and Europe, including one yellow school bus with large black lettering that identified a previous owner as the Huron County School Board. My taxi shared the open road with private cars and official vehicles and government trucks filled with produce and construction materials. I checked into the hotel and immediately hit the streets, walking the now-familiar route down San Rafael Street from the hotel to the city center, along streets I knew as well as many in my own city.

Business Returns to Old Havana

The long walk took me through neighborhoods of two- and three-story apartments and handsome homes with arched doors and windows, ornate iron grillwork, and peeling paint. The streets were lined with cars and motorcycles; people sat on doorsteps and chatted, kids played on the sidewalks, family laughter came from open windows, laundry dried on the ubiquitous balconies, and the sticky-sweet, opulent smell of overripe fruit scented the air. I passed stores and shops in buildings time-dated by their architecture of big picture windows set in aluminum frames and double-entry doors made

1. The "yellow men," so called because they wore yellow jackets. Their job was to stop government vehicles—trucks, official cars, buses, etc.—with space for passengers and assign hitchhikers to that space. The system augmented the country's delapidated and overtaxed bus system.

of oiled wood and glass, doors with brass plates on them where customers could place a hand to push their way inside. I had walked past those stores more times than I could count from memory and had never seen the doors swing open for a single customer, had only seen the stores boarded up and empty, like hollow, dusty reminders of Cuba's neediness. But now they were open for business. I wandered in and out of several of them, where milling customers chatted among themselves, held up merchandise for inspection and approval, and pulled companions to investigate discoveries in the next aisle. Satisfied-looking customers once again browsed and handled the stock, which was mostly small household items and uninspired clothing. Convenience-style stores selling soft drinks, beer, candy, cigarettes, and food had popped up here and there, crowded with Cubans clutching pesos and dollars, eager to spend, eager to buy, happy to be back in the game. The energy of commerce had returned to Havana.

Out on the sidewalks and plazas, hyperbusy men shined shoes, women at card tables glued on false fingernails, and people repaired bicycles and anything else that was broken but salvageable in a country where little was considered beyond reclamation, even disposable cigarette lighters. Long lines of patient customers waited for products and services; the longest was stationed beside a shooting gallery constructed from a sheet-metal backdrop, where kids shot pellet guns at crudely fashioned ducks.

Unusual Business Locations

I stopped to talk with a barber as he worked on a customer who was seated in an old-fashioned barber's chair of cracked brown leather and white enamel. "I live just over there," he said, looking up from his work to point down the street. "Every morning my son helps me carry the chair from the apartment to the sidewalk. This is where I do business," he said, glancing up and down the sidewalk. "My father was a barber. This was his chair. He had it in his own shop with several other barbers. When the shop was closed down, my father kept the chair. He put it in the apartment, where it has been for more than twenty-five years. He cut the hair for family and neighbors. I did the same thing. We had to be careful doing that; now I am doing the same thing on the sidewalk," he said with a Cuban shake of his head. When I asked him why his father had shut his shop, the talkative young barber ignored my foolish question.

After walking nearly to the city center, I grabbed a cab and headed for another piece of familiar ground—the Plaza de la Catedral and the Plaza de las Armas, situated only blocks from each other in La Habana Vieja—eager for the understanding that comes from measuring change against what's familiar. During the previous visits I had spent many hours in these spots, but the lack of energy and action, the subdued presence and promise, had made them seem like emotionally depressed pieces of urban geography compared to what they should have been, what they must have been in earlier decades, so I quit making the trip after a few times. But when the cab dropped me off, I walked the narrow cobbled streets into a reconstituted Havana.

I went into a *paladar*, without a clear idea of what it was—a two-table restaurant set up in the small living room of an apartment, where the family served homemade meals of black beans and rice, a piece of fish or beef, potatoes, beer, and dessert for $2.50. The husband, who acted as host, waiter, janitor, and social critic, told me that during the several months they had been open business had been good, but several recently opened *paladares* had caused him to start worrying about falling profits. I congratulated him on good fortune and his rapid conversion to businesslike anxieties. They had placed no signs on the building; his only advertising consisted of walking the surrounding streets of Old Havana handing out professional-looking business cards to foreigners and leaving the front door of the house open as an invitation, as a sign of their readiness to do business.

Street Artists

Artists and craftsmen had commandeered strategic spots along the sidewalks, in the parks, and in the plazas. Painters in all media and styles—oils, acrylics, and charcoal, from folk art to abstract—displayed their work against the black wrought-iron fences surrounding the plazas and under the protective eaves of the buildings, particularly the Museum of Education with its broad, wide overhang. The open space of the plaza was filled with tables manned by booksellers, crafters of black coral jewelry, skilled carvers of beautifully polished wooden canes and masks, and vendors of revolutionary artifacts, particularly Che's portrait on postcards, pins, posters, and T-shirts. I walked around, gawking and marveling at the new look of the place, crowded, busy, hustling, seductive, like it should be, like it always should have been, like hip locations in other cities, such as Saint-Germain-des-Prés in Paris and Jackson Square in New Orleans, but unlike anything I had ever seen in Havana.

Like street artists everywhere, Havana's eagerly sought customers, but failing the sale they settled for a conversation to pass time. I was drawn to a set of brightly colored folk-art paintings and drifted into conversation with the artist, Francisco, an extra-tall, extra-gaunt Afro-Cuban who bent his head down every time he spoke. He and his friend, Raúl, traveled across Havana every day by bus—a two-hour ride that involved several transfers—from a neighborhood on the road to Varadero Beach. Crowded buses with erratic schedules made it difficult for them to arrive early enough to secure a good spot, preferably under the protective care of the museum, away from the threat of sun and rain.

When I told Francisco how struck I was by the changes in the area, he said, "There are other places where people sell things for dollars outdoors. We come here because it's the closest one to our home." He wrote out directions to other locations where the underground economy was merging with the official one, creating something new that was feeling its way, still pretty awkward and sometimes messy.

Street Hustlers

Arts and crafts attracted tourists, who attracted *jineteros* [street hustlers] and black marketeers, who staked out turf and worked to establish their reputations. Pointing to a discrete young man with a fixed smile, Raúl said, "He's Old Havana's most reliable source of Cuban cigars. Very honest. Never sells fakes. Has fair prices. He's the man you should see if you want cigars. He has good contacts inside the factory"—the ultimate certification of a black marketeer's credibility. Raúl pointed out another man known for providing "companionship" and a third for operating an unofficial taxi service: "He uses his father's car and is very good. Knows the streets of Havana and is cheap and a safe driver, not at all dangerous."

A woman rolls cigars in her family's shop. In 1993 the Cuban government began allowing Cubans to establish their own small businesses.

In his whispering style, Francisco said serious problems developed when it first became legal for the artists and vendors to set up for business. It took some time for the artists and the illegals to work out a streetwise etiquette concerning the tourists, upon whom everyone so depended. "Some of the *jineteros* would come up and start talking to tourists while they were looking at my paintings, trying to take them away. It was really bad," he said. "Some of those guys were really rude. Now it doesn't happen very often." The new protocol called for black marketeers to stay clear of the tourists while they browsed among the artists and craftsmen, but once outside selling range they became a fair target.

I stood a long time talking with Francisco and Raúl, surrounded by their art under the wide overhang in front of the Museum of Education. The friends shared a knowing laugh when I asked for details about the black market. "There is no black market; it's the Cuban business. It's all the same now. Everything is dollars," they explained. "Everything."

The Rise of a Dollar Economy

What previously had been underground and dangerous had in recent months become open and hopeful. A series of decrees issued during the summer and fall of 1993, and another in the fall of 1994, made it legal for Cubans to possess dollars and to open shops offering goods and services. Everyone who wanted to do business, from artists to manicurists—some fifty thousand Cubans by early 1994—paid 45 pesos to the Comité de Finanzas to acquire a state license of operation; the licenses were easy to get, with the single important qualifying question being *Where did you get the tools and materials?* The only reasonable answer, which was never given, was *Stolen from the state.* Everyone ignored the obvious, and dollars had pumped the juice back into Havana's streets, dropping the black market exchange rate from 120 pesos to the dollar to 50, causing many Cubans for a short time to believe that it was smarter to hold pesos over dollars.

The switch to dollars changed the lives of Cubans. Francisco and Raúl and their companions along the plaza could openly sell their art for profit and make a living from their hard work and talent. "This is the first time we can make money," explained Francisco. "Before, if an artist had an exhibition, even in Mexico or some place like that, the money went to the state. The government gave us some of it, but who knows? No one ever thought it was enough. Not for what was sold." With the single decree that legalized dollars, artists emerged from the shadows of Cuban society into the open space of the plazas, selling their own art and pocketing the cash directly. In a society where a physician earned 500 to 600 pesos per month, $25 per painting gave Francisco an economic edge; even at 50 pesos to the dollar, the math made selling art on the street quite appealing compared to a state job.

Francisco's paintings were dramatically colored and folk-primitive in style, hinting of Haitian influence. Set outdoors amid the vivid greenery of a Caribbean landscape, several pieces told tales of Santería [a Cuban religion with African origins] ceremonies, in which dancers and drummers made offerings to the *orishas*, the Santería gods, offerings of chickens, pigeons, eggs, pastries, and candles, as the religious tradition demands. The scenes were festive and joyous; the figures were all black. One two-painting set depicted the story of a man on horseback luring away a resting man's wife, and of the husband trying to reclaim his mate, all the while the *orishas* looked on, laughing, mocking, sequestered among the trees in a shroud of pale orange that contrasted against the green of the trees and the blue of the sky. The conflict expressed in the two paintings was left unresolved. I asked Francisco, "Is the struggle in those paintings supposed to represent life in contemporary Cuba? You know, conflicting loyalties?"

"I am not that clever," he said with a laugh. "My paintings would be well-known stories to any Cuban of color. Most of them come from tales we all heard from our grandparents, in our childhood. Stories that are as familiar to us as our lives."

A Loss of Politeness

Hanging out and talking with Francisco and Raúl gave me the impression that Cuba was healing herself in small ways. But the streets always kept my enthusiasm in check. During my first visit to Cuba, in 1991, Caputo the photographer had remarked that savvy Africa watchers considered the black market exchange rate a good indication of a nation's stability, or instability, as the case may be. In Cuba, I had come to think that it might be more accurate, or at least more interesting, to judge the fitness of the society by watching the *jineteros*, those people on the fringes of society who hustled foreigners.

Whatever the utility of that theory, for the first time I felt flashes of uneasiness on the streets, brought on by the growing number and determined manner of the men who tried to make contact, to start the conversation they hoped would lead to a deal of some sort. Impossible to ignore and difficult to send away, they seemed more aggressive than I remembered. One *jinetero* told me that he was a prizefighter, as he shadowboxed beside me down the sidewalk near the Habana Libre Hotel; another boasted he was a karate expert; and a third claimed he was a Tae Kwon Do instructor as he fell in step with me outside the Hotel Inglaterra. Finally it came to me—this was tough-guy street hustling Cuban style, not with knives or guns, not even with threats or intimidation, but with information so vague, so implicit, that it took me time to realize they were suggesting danger without actually threatening anyone. Very Cuban. However harmless and quaint these episodes seemed upon reflection, there was no denying that persistence had displaced politeness, that subtlety and charm were disappearing along with an equal portion of the lightheartedness that had made Havana such an appealing destination.

A Doctor Turned *Jinetero*

Late one night I left the Plaza de la Catedral with a man who offered taxi service to my hotel. As we walked across the square to his car he introduced himself as a doctor and presented his card with the promise to treat me for free if I needed medical services. The taxi turned out to be a private car doubling as a nighttime cab, a practice that had grown common in Havana from the time Cubans could have dollars. With a man driving and a women sitting in the passenger seat, my doctor friend began his pitch as soon as the cramped, faded sedan started moving.

I politely responded to all his offers, one after another. *Yes, the woman in the front is very beautiful, but I do not wish her as a companion for the evening. Yes, I am certain you can get me drugs and your PCG will keep me as hard as a man could imagine for the longest time, but I do not want any, even if it will lower my cholesterol as well.* And on it went, with offers of cigars, bicycles, and a handsome exchange rate.

We headed off in the general direction of the hotel, but not by a route that could be considered direct, even in the most flexible definition of the term. The price of the ride was preset, so why would they be stretching out the drive? In hopes of creating a possibility? Perhaps. But a possibility for what? I wondered. Illegal business, without a doubt, but maybe with larceny as an alternative? Brand new at being small-time hustlers, they didn't seem to be able to get it right. What the fuck, I thought, was I going to get mugged in Havana by a doctor, a hooker, and their driver? It didn't seem likely, but with everything in Havana changing, anything seemed possible. I pushed the situation off center by suggesting that I might need to hire a car the next day, which picked up everyone's mood—and the driver's sense of direction. Upon our arrival at the hotel, the doctor got terribly agitated when I refused to give him my name and room number, no matter how hard he insisted—and insist he did, until I thought he might stamp his foot in frustration like a petulant child. Nothing was going as he had planned, so he gave up, returned to the car in a huff, and slammed the door. The vehicle sped off as I turned toward the sanctuary of the hotel lobby, walking past a watchful audience of curious Cubans who had gathered on the sidewalk to see how the show would end.

Making Ends Meet During the "Special Period"

Tony Mendoza

After Soviet aid dried up in 1991 (when the USSR col-
lapsed), the Cuban economy was in dire straits. The government tried to encourage tourism and allowed greater economic freedoms to the Cuban population—anything to bring
money into the country during the so-called "Special Period"
of the 1990s.

During the Special Period, private individuals such as
artists and artisans were permitted to sell their wares directly
to foreign tourists. This was quite a concession since Cuban
socialism frowned on entrepreneurialism. One by-product of
this arrangement to accommodate tourism was the *jineteros*
and *jineteras*. Literally translated from the Spanish as "jock-
eys," these male and female street hustlers sold Cuban-made
goods, especially high-quality rum and cigars, on the black
market for dollars. Many of the young, attractive *jineteros*
and *jineteras* also prostituted themselves for payment in
American dollars.

Tony Mendoza was born in Cuba to a well-to-do Cuban
family. In 1960, at age eighteen, he and his family fled Castro's Cuba and settled in the United States; he eventually
became a professor of photography at Ohio State University.
In 1996 he returned to visit his boyhood home and to take
photographs for a book about Cuba. In this excerpt he relates

his conversations with a *jinetera* and a self-employed fisherman, and discovers that socialism had never quite stamped
out entrepreneurialism on the island.

The best-paid self-employed workers in Cuba are the
jineteras. In the old days, prostitutes were called *putas*,
but that word had a seedy and dishonorable connotation.
Jineteras are never called that. *Jineteras* are different. They
have college degrees. Their activity is seen by Cubans as an
entrepreneurial activity, as opposed to a vice. If a *jinetera*
has a "date" every night she could make $2,000 a month tax
free, which in Cuba is a fortune; thus the temptation is high.
A brain surgeon would have to do brain surgery in Cuba for
eight years to earn an equivalent amount.

The Changing Character of the Revolution

Fidel never tires of repeating in his speeches how the Yankees had transformed prerevolutionary Cuba into their gambling den and their brothel and how the elimination of casinos and prostitution during the first days of 1959 was a
testament to the high moral character of the Revolution. Now
times are different. I saw *jineteras* everywhere in Havana, always dressed in black, like New York artists, and I didn't see
any getting arrested. I'm assuming that the high moral character of the Revolution has come down quite a few notches
because Cuba desperately needs the tourists and their dollars. I got the strong impression that tourism in Cuba is pre-
dominantly sex tourism. What I suspect really bothers the
government is the fact that the *jineteras*, the highest-earning
self-employed individuals in Cuba, cannot be taxed as every
other self-employed worker is taxed, because the *jineteras*
are illegal and therefore don't officially exist. I wondered
how Fidel was dealing with this moral quandary and the
flowering of prostitution in the Havana of the Special Period.
I expected him to rationalize it somehow, but I didn't expect
him to say this, in a July 12, 1992, speech:

We had to accept tourism as an economic need, but we said that

it will be tourism free of drugs, free of brothels, free of prostitu-
tion, free of gambling. There is no cleaner, purer tourism than
Cuba's tourism, because there is really no drug trafficking, no
gambling houses. There are hookers, but prostitution is not al-
lowed in our country. There are no women forced to sell them-
selves to a man, to a foreigner, to a tourist. Those who do so do it
on their own, voluntarily, and without any need for it. We can say
that they are highly educated hookers and quite healthy, because
we are the country with the lowest number of AIDS cases. There
are nearby countries which have tens of thousands of AIDS cases.
Therefore, there is truly no tourism healthier than Cuba's.

Everybody Knows

Jineteras accosted me every day, and I had a standard reply:
"Sorry," I'd say, showing my wedding band, "but I'm married."

"So what, that's no reason. Your wife will never find out."

"Yes she will. My wife has extrasensory perception.
She'll know." Still, I wanted to know how these women felt
about what they were doing.

I was eating dinner at the *paladar* [a restaurant operated
in the owner's home]. Three Italian men came in with their
Cuban companions. They got a large table near my table,
and the three men sat together at one end of the table and
spoke in Italian to each other. The women were ignored.
They sat at the other end of the table and talked among
themselves. My table was near this group, so I moved my
chair closer to the women and started a conservation. The
Italian men didn't seem to mind. I learned that the women
earned from twenty-five to fifty dollars an evening, but included in the deal was the dinner, and afterward they'd go
dancing. They saw it as a date with a fifty-dollar tip. One of
the women in the group was finishing her medical intern-
ship. She said it was very tempting to earn fifty dollars in
one night, eat a good dinner, talk to foreigners, find out how
the rest of the world lives, have fun. She could buy whatever
she wanted and help her family. I asked her if her parents
knew what she did to earn those dollars.

"Of course they know. How else in Cuba am I going to

make this kind of money and buy the things we are buying?
I don't tell them the details, but they know."

"Are they upset?"

"Not really. *Hay que resolver* [one does what one must].
I'm supporting the entire family."

"Aren't you afraid of AIDS?" "No. There is no AIDS in
Cuba. I wouldn't dream of having sex without a condom.
Nobody here does it without condoms."

"So, what do you think about the Revolution?" I asked her.
She looked at me as if I were from Mars.

"You still talk about the Revolution? I don't talk about
that. It bores me. I'm not interested in that."

Diving for Money

There are many unusual self-employment categories, such
as the people who set up a table and chair on the sidewalk
and offer a service that must be unique to Cuba—filling up
cigarette lighters. One day I discovered a still more unique
and decidedly macabre way to earn a living. My apartment
building was two blocks from the Malecón, and every morning I went to the seawall. A man sold coffee there, and I
liked to start my day sitting on the seawall, drinking coffee
and staring at the ocean. I noticed a man equipped with fins,
mask, and snorkel, a spear gun, and a tiny buoy trailing behind him, swimming straight out every morning until he disappeared. I used to spear fish, so I was very interested in
what he was doing. One day I caught him before he went
out. He was an impressive looking fifty-five-year-old man,
with long white hair, a carefully trimmed beard, and a
bronzed, muscular body.

"I see you swimming out every morning. How far do you
go?"

"Depends. Some days I snorkel by the wall. What I do is
I retrieve fish hooks, nylons, which I sell. When I go for fish
I swim out seven miles. At other times, I go looking for bod-
ies. I find bodies even further out, ten miles out."

"Did you say bodies?"

"Yes, for example. When people left on rafts and they

were unlucky, a storm got them, and they drowned. Remember the rafters? Many left, but many ended in the sea. Many took necklaces, rings, money—I've found wallets with two thousand dollars underwater."

"Why do you find the bodies ten miles out? Did a boat sink there?"

"No. Between Varadero and Camarioca there is a trench, about ten miles out. Rafters who drown at sea get brought back by the current and they get caught in this trench. I dive down there for the jewelry and the wallets. I find gold medallions, rings, and I sell them."

"Don't bodies float?"

"When the lungs fill up with water they sink. Usually I only find the skeletons. And the rings are still there."

"So the fish eat them?"

"Well I've seen a leg in one place, a head in another. Lately there haven't been too many rafters since the U.S. started returning them. So I've been going fishing."

Out Where the Fish Are

"You say you go out seven miles. Why?"

"That's where the fish are. The shore is fished out. Also, all the fish by the Malecón are polluted. Where I get them, they are clean. The place I go to, a reef, it's only 100, 120 feet deep. It takes me about 40 seconds to go down, and I stay down looking for fish for a minute. I used to last 3 minutes when I was young, but now I'm only good for 2, 2½ minutes."

"What happens if a boat sees you out there by yourself, seven miles out?"

"They usually slow down and take pictures."

"Aren't you afraid when you are out there far from shore, alone, without a raft? What if you get a cramp?"

"No, I believe in destiny. I'm going to die when destiny decides."

"But aren't you increasing your odds? Aren't you afraid of running into a huge shark?"

"No. I know sharks. They don't bother me. Sharks are afraid of sounds. Sometimes they swim around me, and if I want to get rid of them all I do is tap my knife quickly against the gun. They hate that metallic sound and they take off. If I'm close to shore and I see a shark I see only one thing—a big dollar sign. I'll shoot him and try to bring him in. People here eat shark."

"Are there any Great Whites here?"

"No, no, that's our salvation! They don't come here. No, I'm never scared at sea. I'll tell you this. The way I feel in the sea, when I'm out there five or six hours off the coast, I feel at peace, because I'm among beings that love me, that give me life. I'm more scared when I get on land. People, I don't understand them. They do strange things, they say strange things, I look at their faces and they look terrible. I don't know what's happening, I don't understand humanity. I don't want to talk to people. They look at you and say things that aren't true. Sincerely, I feel much better with the fish in the ocean than with people on land. They are the ones that give me life. They are the ones that help me."

Young People Express Their Disillusionment with Socialism

Andrei Codrescu

> During the Special Period in the 1990s, Castro attempted to make up for the loss of trade with the Socialist nations of Europe by encouraging foreign tourists to visit Cuba. As tourists began to arrive in greater numbers, they made it possible for Cubans to augment their incomes by providing them with a variety of goods and services, legal and illegal. Ironically, by coming into closer contact with foreigners, almost all of whom were well-off financially, young Cubans became increasingly disillusioned with socialism and longed to live in a country where they could more easily accumulate the material goods that were missing in Socialist Cuba.
>
> Andrei Codrescu is a Romanian-American journalist. In 1997 he and two companions traveled to Cuba to see the country firsthand. In this excerpt, Codrescu and his mates make the acquaintance of two *jineteros*, young street hustlers who make a living by selling goods and services to tourists, who take them on a tour of Havana's slums. During the tour, the *jineteros* make it clear that they and most young Cubans are tired of socialism and are eager to leave Cuba.

In front of the Capri, the *jineteros* were thick, more *jineteros* than *jineteras* this time, maybe because the girls worked in the daytime in offices and factories. When we exited the Capri, two skinny kids accosted us. One of them spoke English: "Where are you from? Spain? Italy? Estados Unidos? Wow! My dad is a Marielito—he lives in Miami. We talk on the phone. My English pretty good, no? You like my English? I go to tourism school. That man"—long-beard gesture [symbolizing Castro]—"is crazy. He drive us all crazy. You don't [know] how poor is poor. You want to see a Cuban market? Shit. You want to see the girl place? The drug place? The church place?"

Art and David were ignoring the *jinetero*, but I was interested. His English really was pretty good, and his non-stop patter was full of nuggets of articulate social criticism. He had a gold tooth that flashed in his intelligent-looking chocolate face like a lighthouse signal. He said his name was Pablo, and that his friend was Luis. I shook their hands.

"Things will be shit for another twenty years," Pablo said, and made the air-beard gesture again. I handed him and his friend Luis some money and some of my baseball pencils. Pablo refused at first, then said: "You have to come to my house, you have to see how Luis lives. Real Cuba. Not that propaganda."

We were walking along, David snapping pictures, Art taping street sounds, the *jineteros* hot on our heels.

Pablo said: "Cubans have a lot of rights. You know what they are? Education, health, housing, and stealing from the state."

I laughed. Our second Cuban joke.

Pablo pointed to a camel-bus with people hanging outside from the door. "Crazy transport. I go in there, I steal something from somebody, somebody steals something from me. By the time you get off, you stole your stuff back."

A Tour of the Havana Slums

I wasn't sure this was a joke, but I thought, "Third joke," anyway.

After some hesitation by my companions (Ariel [the author's official tour guide] was not with us this morning), I decided that we ought to take Pablo up on his offer to show us where he lives, the "real Cuba." If this had been New York and a fast-talking hustler had decided to take us to, let's say, Harlem, I might have had second thoughts. But I'd heard that Cuba had little violent crime (a claim rejected later, emphatically, by people who knew) and decided to take a chance.

The section of Central Havana where the taxi deposited the five of us was even more sinister looking than the missed-goat neighborhood. It was a maze of ruins of nineteenth-century buildings that once must have looked Parisian. They were called *solares*, because they were mostly roofless and the tropical sun came in unobstructed. Up to ten people lived in each one-room apartment. Every entrance twisted into a dark alley leading to makeshift cubicles, rickety stairs. Shirtless men cooked on ancient gas stoves, women nursed babies under the glow of small TVs, toothless old people mumbled in the dark.

Luis and Pablo's one-room home stank like frying fat, pigs, chickens, and shit. It opened into a small cement court-yard overhung with laundry. A roofless kitchen was at the end. Fat bubbled in a pot.

"You want to see the bathroom?" Pablo grinned with in-explicable delight. I took one look at the foul-smelling hole in the ground with a bucket next to it and beat a retreat. We were introduced to Pablo's mother and grandmother, and an angry-looking teenager. A baby who was either asleep or dead—he didn't stir during the entire visit—lay in a stroller covered up. Pablo said, "It's my baby, his mother is Luis's sister, she's here somewhere."

She appeared later, a tough-looking teenager, and said, "I'm taking the baby to the doctor." But an hour later, the baby was still there, the mother nowhere in sight.

How Poor Cubans Survive

I interviewed Pablo by the boiling clothes in the back. I asked him how the family survived.

"You have six pounds of rice a month. A few pounds of sugar. No potatoes. Eggs, you know. We have seven eggs a month. Milk is only for children to seven years old, you know."

"So what do you do about that?"

"We go into the street, talk to the tourist. We try to live, without fooling the tourist."

I had my doubts about this, but let it pass.

"The girls are out there working," I said.

"We are in trouble. They sells their body. They don't know what they do. You go on the Malecón Avenue at nine o'clock. You see the girls. Yes, we have problems, we have no money, nothing to do, you know?"

"You're speaking honestly."

"I'm not afraid. Many things we can't talk about. We only have two TV channels, only the communist newspaper. They speak a lot of shits about the U.S.A."

"Do most young people feel the way you do?"

"Ninety percent do. Only the old people who fought in Revolution feel other. But nothing gonna change, nothing gonna happen. In kindergarten we sang songs about the Revolution." Pablo pulled out his wallet and showed me his ID. "This is when you were born, your mother, your photo, and here it says, 'Skin color, *mulato.*' That's all who I am."

"Your skin. I thought your color didn't matter in Cuba."

"It's lies. Black is poor."

"What are you going to do?"

"Get the hell out of this country. Everybody wants to. We look at the water every day. Every day I see a boat, a tire, a piece of wood . . . out of here."

Pablo was a gumbo of bravura and contradictions, and I had a feeling that we were nowhere near the bottom of the pot. Politics was, of course, one commodity. Another was about to appear.

Buying Stolen Cigars

"You want to buy cigars? Luis's uncle steals them from the factory direct."

"How much are these cigars?" David asked. He was interested. He was getting quite a taste for Cuban cigars.

"It depends how many boxes you going to buy. If you buy five boxes, maybe the price is going down. We try to live.

It's like *paladares*, you know."

Paladares were the new private businesses allowed in Cuba. Small restaurants, tiny hotels. The restaurants were allowed only five tables, and were forbidden to serve beef, shrimp, or lobster, which were state monopolies. The hotels were also restricted to five rooms and couldn't serve food. But licensed *paladares* paid half their earnings to the government. I doubted that Pablo had any such intentions.

"Okay. Let me see the Monte Cristos."

Luis disappeared through a hole in the back wall and was gone for about twenty minutes. During that time we

"There's No Future in Cuba"

The Special Period was brought on by the collapse of communism in Europe. Thus deprived of its best trading partners and Soviet aid, the Cuban economy went into a tailspin. Young people were particularly disillusioned by this economic decline, as they had no memory of living conditions in prerevolutionary Cuba. Biographer Robert E. Quirk relates how Castro outlined some new sacrifices that would have to be made to cope with the situation in 1991. As Quirk notes, young people responded with very little enthusiasm to Castro's declarations.

Fidel Castro responded [to the collapse of European communism] by declaring a national state of emergency—a "special period" in the time of peace. "Long live rigidity!" he exclaimed. He saw the strong likelihood that fuel supplies would be diminished, if not eliminated. For years, he said, the revolutionary government had developed plans in the event of a military invasion. Now those plans would be implemented. He would allow no compromises. If necessary, the country would revert to a subsistence economy, the primitivism of the preindustrial age. He spoke of a "zero option." Factories would shut down. Thousands of city dwellers would be moved to the countryside. Oxen would replace tractors. Windmills could provide electricity. The people would ride bicycles, instead of buses or private vehicles. Castro tried crouched in the dark room, flies buzzing around us, the baby not moving. The sound of fights, broken glass, and a baseball game on the radio provided Pablo with background for his nonstop patter. His subject was Cuba, and he wanted us to know all about it, because he thought about it all the time.

"All these people crowded here are from Oriente, the East. People here in Havana hate these people from Santiago, it's like Bosnia and Herzegovina, we call them Palestinians." There are no precise figures on how many people are now living illegally in Havana, but some estimates put the number of *"palestinos"* at 400,000.

to cast the events in the best possible light. "Could anything be more healthy?" he asked. He seemed to be enjoying the spectacle. "Someday we might be thankful for this special situation. We are going back to the ox, the noble ox." If the ground was wet, he explained, tractors were useless. Oxen were thirteen times as productive. They did not require spare parts. As he spoke, he chopped the air with his fists. "We don't care who or what falls from power anywhere, but here nothing is going to fall!" Let the Yankees dream their foolish dreams. No one in Cuba would surrender. . . .

But as Castro dwelt on the prospects in subsequent months, young Cubans worried that he was leading them to the edge of an abyss. Part of a postrevolutionary generation, they were unmoved by his antiquated rhetoric, redolent of the Sierra Maestra days [the early days of the Revolution]. They no longer volunteered for work in the fields or overseas. Many had no prospects of jobs, and thousands of soldiers were being brought back from Africa as the fighting ended in Angola. A popular singer told Andres Oppenheimer, a reporter for the *Miami Herald*, that young people were tired of being treated as though they were stupid. "We're not being listened to," he said. A grizzled veteran of the Sierra Maestra campaigns lamented: "Hope? I need a candle to look for hope here. There's no future in Cuba."

Robert E. Quirk, *Fidel Castro*. New York: W.W. Norton, 1993.

Over and over, Pablo returned to the Bearded One, whose name he never mentioned, only making the beard sign with his hand. After a particularly inspired diatribe, he fell silent for a brief moment, then mused, in flagrant contradiction to what he'd just said: "He's not a bad guy, you know. He wants the best for Cuba. But you know who stops him?"

I had an idea.

"The communists! If he could, he would. But the communists, they criminals."

I wondered just how magnetic Fidel's draw must be if, after all these years, he still managed to somehow project himself outside the system he'd created. But Pablo wasn't wrong. In his speeches, Fidel cleverly blamed the Party for failures, and hinted that things might have been different if his authority had been unhindered.

Luis returned with four beautiful boxes. In the stark room, the cigars shone incongruously in their luxurious silver tubes. David admired their individual cedar-leaf wrappings and inhaled their deep, fine tobacco aroma. A beautiful box of Romeo y Julietas beckoned to him. Luis had labels, too, to glue the boxes shut so they looked factory-new. He also provided a receipt he insisted would keep the Cubans from confiscating them at the border.

"These are three hundred dollars at the store!" exclaimed Pablo. We worked out a $120 price and the box of twenty-five was ours. This transaction, of course, was precisely the kind of thing every guidebook advises against. Do not buy cigars on the street, they warn, they are phony. But David swore that they were just fine. Only later, when we actually bought some from the cigar factory, the same box was $25. This was one of the many ways in which our fixer, Pablo, worked out his fee. . . .

A Cuban Open-Air Market

[Pablo] took us down some alley at the end of which a sorry assortment of rickety tables held shriveled black bananas, some grotesquely huge manioc roots, piles of little potatoes. A man was butchering an animal and dropping bloody hunks of meat on a dirty stone table. Swarms of flies buzzed over it and a crowd clamored like the flies around the meat, but nobody was buying.

"Dollars," said Pablo, "all cost dollars. Nobody has dollars."

The private markets, Pablo explained, were run by the army, which alone had the trucks to transport the peasants and their produce to city markets. In exchange, they got half the profits. In addition to being in private business, Castro's army, the largest standing army in Latin America, was well fed compared to the rest of the people. The soldiers had no need for clothes, either, since they wore state-issued uniforms. A military business-state might well follow socialism in Cuba.

I thanked Pablo for the tour of his world. I was anxious to get back to the hotel to take a shower. . . . Pablo was astounded at this early departure. "This is only beginning. I show you more Cuba. You want to go to drug place? Marijuana? Cocaína? Heroin? We have all in Havana. I show you the girls, the boys, what you like."

It was hard convincing him that we soft Yankees cannot endure too many sensations all at once. I slipped him forty dollars, but he waved my hand away. "Now we see really interesting things." I insisted he take the money and, finally, he did. We shook hands. . . .

Avoiding Arrest

"How do you stay away from the police?" I asked him.

He laughed. "The police has to live, man. You give him a dollar." Then he became wistful. "Not always. Me and Luis went to jail maybe six times. Everybody go to jail. If I buy at the private market, come home with the package of maybe meat for my mother, milk for the baby, the policeman ask for receipt. No receipt, he take you to jail. You give him money, he take the package, bastard still take you to jail.". . .

I asked him: "What do you think you'll be doing in the future? Do you have plans for the future?"

"In all the ways, take off from Cuba, you know? I don't want to live in Cuba. If Cuba change, you need a lot of money to make something, make some business. Make something. In many ways, we need to take off. Here will be crazy. Maybe we have war inside. I don't know. I don't want to stay here, okay? It's my opinion. I don't know other people. I'm not too intelligent, but I try to be intelligent, you know? I try to learn in life. Not everything is the money, but we need the money. For that reason, you need to take off. Because people without money are nothing. You can see. It's crazy." He laughed again, a laugh too wise for his years.

It was crazy, all right: Not everything is money. People without money are nothing. Has anyone put it better? Pablo surely was one of a kind. But I had the feeling the slums of Cuba teemed with young men who thought the way he did.

This was Cuba now: poised precariously between the lost utopia and the unpolished hustle.

Older People Speak Up for Fidel

Christopher Hunt

After 1990, the Cuban economy generally was unable to provide most Cubans with the luxuries of life. Sometimes it could not provide them with the basic necessities. This situation caused much disillusionment and discontent with Castro and socialism among Cubans too young to remember life before the revolution. Older people, however, had a better awareness of the sweeping changes that Castro had brought to Cuba, and many were grateful to him for implementing those changes.

Christopher Hunt is an American journalist who went to Cuba in 1995 in the hope of meeting Castro. While there, he traveled the length of the island and spoke with dozens of ordinary Cubans. In this excerpt, he relates his conversations with several older people in the town square of Santiago de Cuba, the island's second largest city. They tell him that, although things are bad with Castro, without him they might very well be worse.

"**F**idel was up there."

Juan pointed north, toward the two-story structure across the street from the park where we sat. As long as the city block, the building's fresh white paint and smooth tiles stood out in Santiago's faded downtown. Through the ground floor's arched doorway were the offices of the Poder Popular, the People's Power. Attached to the face of the city hall's second floor were three wooden balconies, painted blue.

"He was on the balcony," said the aging Cuban, indicating the center of the building. "The people were all around here. Everywhere."

The sweep of Juan's gesture covered the whole of Céspedes Park. Halfway up the hill separating Santiago de Cuba's horseshoe-shaped harbor and the edge of the downtown district at Martí Plaza, the square had long been the home of the city's power brokers. The first was Diego Velázquez, the Spanish conquistador who established Santiago de Cuba, Havana, and five other settlements. Built in 1522, the stone house from which he ruled the island still occupied half of the park's west edge.

The Catholic Church set up shop on the south side of the square. On a base above street level, the cathedral had twin towers flanking a domed center. Its wooden doors looked too heavy to open. A different sort of clout resided a quarter turn counterclockwise. Converted to a cultural center, an elegant building had once been a club for merchants and landowners. Beside it stood a hotel.

The Joy of Liberation

The park's shaded benches began filling up late in the afternoon. Old men came to pass the time in groups of four or five. Women brought their children to play on the broad walkways. University students favored the edge nearest the cultural center. Guitarists, alone and in pairs, strummed too softly to disturb the calm, which made it hard to picture the contrasting scene described by Juan.

"It was madness. The park was full. Full! So many people I couldn't count them. And not just in the park. All the streets were full. And people were cheering. I was cheering too. The joy that I felt was the greatest of my life."

"Your whole life?"

"Greater than the day I married. Greater than the day my son was born."

The previous night, [Cuban dictator Fulgencio] Batista decided that his 46,000-man army was no match for a few thousand bearded rebels and fled Havana with his wife, three children, and enough money to last a lifetime. Receiving the news at the sugar mill where he was spending New Year's Eve, Castro left to "liberate" Santiago de Cuba. Other guerrillas streamed down from the mountains. The victors reached the city in the wee hours of January 2, 1959.

Santiago de Cuba was wide awake. Too excited to change out of pajamas and hairnets, residents lined the streets to cheer the arrival of the men who toppled the tyrant. Not everybody could fit into Céspedes Park. Those who managed to squeeze in saw Fidel Castro appear, like a messiah, on the balcony to deliver his first speech as the leader of Cuba.

"What did he say?"

"I don't remember. It was enough just to see him."

"But why?"

"I wasn't a *communista*," said Juan. "But I was a *Fidelista.*"

Life After the Revolution

How long did the spell last? Having seen bits of Juan's life in the days since our first meeting, I reckoned the sixty-year-old had scratched his name from the list of Fidel's fans. First, there was his job. A retired professor, Juan received a pitiful pension. To make ends meet, he went into business with his sister, who lived in the countryside. She brought fresh eggs to the city, where Juan sold them to friends and neighbors.

Split two ways, weekly profits of about a hundred and fifty pesos didn't buy luxury. Juan invited me to visit his home, five blocks from Céspedes Park. Five steps up from the sidewalk, the front door opened to a living room furnished with three lawn chairs, a record player, and a stack of vinyl disks. A velvet portrait of a ship passing through a canal covered most of one wall. Opposite was a poster of a woman in a swimsuit.

Crowding was a bigger problem than decor. Up a concrete staircase from the living room lived one son, his wife, and their four-year-old boy. Their bedroom provided the only access to a second bedroom, which housed another son, an engineer who worked in a hotel, plus his wife and infant.

On the ground floor, a doorless room occupied by the daughter's family provided access to the bedroom of the master, who slept beside the kitchen. An ancient woman and the fifty-year-old daughter with whom she shared a double bed in the back brought the tally to thirteen.

"Can't your children get their own homes?" I asked.

"There's no money to build new homes," said Juan.

We left the claustrophobic quarters and walked a block to the bodega, where a crowd of twenty waited their turn to buy subsidized groceries. *"¿El último?"* ["Who's last in line?"] asked Juan. A position established, the Cuban settled on the sidewalk opposite the rations store. The tedium of waiting was broken by a voluminous black woman who screamed "Fuck," "Asshole," "Whore," and curses I hadn't yet learned at the toothless biddy who disputed her place in the line.

Juan didn't gripe about the line. Nor did he complain about the quantity of food provided by the government, which failed to deliver two pounds of the previous month's sugar ration. I heard not one moan about the crowding in his home. Incredulous at his composure, I prodded Juan to comment on his life.

"I feel rich," he said. "The cost of living in Cuba is very low. I own my home. Even if I didn't, the rent to the government is very low. I need only twenty pesos per month to buy food with the ration book. With my supplementary income I can buy extra food at the market. I don't have much money. But in the Cuban system, one doesn't need much money. I have everything I need."

The Benefits of the System

Cuba's system had other fans in Céspedes Park, where I spent a week of afternoons engaged in Santiago de Cuba's favorite pastimes, ducking the sun and shooting the breeze. Tentative at first, I discovered just how little it took to start a conversation. "Hot day" never failed. "The Struggle" earned bonus points. Saying nothing worked too: a lone foreigner was a magnet for a local with time to kill.

The attraction intensified the moment I revealed my roots.

The retired men circled around to pose their backlog of queries about life in the United States. "Does everybody have a car?" was a common question. So were "Is it too dangerous to go out after dark?" and "Do you own a gun?" My failure to explain snow, a wonder Cubans had seen on television, didn't diminish my expert status.

I had a question of my own. I looked at a man old enough for his first gray hairs but too young to spend the rest of his days in a shady park and said, "You aren't working?"

"I'm sick." He held up his left hand. The thumb and index finger were intact. The other three digits had been reduced to stumps. A carpenter, Luis said that seven months had passed since his buzzsaw snapped and mangled his hand. The pain, said the amputee, was the worst of his life. Or so he thought until the doctors reversed their prediction that the fingers could be reattached. He suffered throbbing depression until another solution surfaced.

"They are going to give me new fingers," said Luis.

The news surprised me. Expensive in the free world, prosthetic fingers seemed beyond the means of a poor country's medical system. But Cuba's cash-strapped doctors had a cheaper way to put the carpenter back to work. The following month, Luis was due for an operation that promised to replace the missing fingers with digits lopped off the hand of a dead man.

"And you don't have to pay?"

"In Cuba, hospitals are free."

An older man named Tomás was more explicit about his gratitude to the system built by Castro. Dressed in a plain white shirt and polyester slacks, the pudgy park dweller beckoned for me to join him on a bench. Was it true what they said? Was I really an American? Tomás spent a half-hour describing a poor boy's lifelong fascination with a land that seemed infinitely rich.

"Do you know anything about medicine?" he asked.

"Not much."

"I'm going to tell you something. In 1981 I had cancer." He pointed to the base of his neck. "I went to a good hospital, with good doctors. Cuban doctors. They operated. I had cobalt treatment. Thanks to the Revolution, I'm alive."

Tomás named another debt to his president. Nearly twenty when Castro stood on the balcony overlooking our spot in the park, he had never gone to high school. But schools built in the years that followed assured an education to all. Proud of his country as well as his offspring, Tomás told me that his children held university degrees. Two worked as veterinarians. The other was a translator. But for the Revolution, all three would have been field or factory workers.

The retired laborer asked me to take a look at the scene around us. I saw boredom. Blank stares were the order of the day for the people in Céspedes Park. Recreational arguments only occasionally broke the tedium under the trees. Tomás saw something else. He pointed to a pair of policemen scolding a teenager for resting his feet on a bench.

"Before the Revolution, that boy would have been afraid of the police. They would arrest him, beat him. But not anymore." Pleased with his first point, Tomás made a second one. "The city used to be full of prostitutes. And gambling. Fidel cleaned the city. He made Santiago de Cuba a beautiful place again."

I reminded Tomás about the dire present. What about the shortages of power, water, and housing? What about food rations that left stomachs rumbling? Grown men begged for soap. I told him about a long conversation with a furloughed laborer. That talk ended with the news that it was his birthday. Opening his identity card as proof, he asked for a present, my socks.

"My socks!" I said. "Can Fidel be doing a good job if a man begs for my socks?"

"In thirty-seven years, a man will have good years and bad years," said Tomás.

"Which is this?"

"Bad. But Fidel is a good man. He brought democracy to Cuba."

"Democracy?"

"Fidel is for the people."

Chronology

1933
The Revolt of the Sergeants brings down the Machado government.

1940
Cuba adopts a new constitution that incorporates a number of liberal reforms in politics and economics.

1952
Fulgencio Batista takes control of the government and suspends the 1940 constitution.

1953
Fidel Castro leads an attack on the Moncada barracks in Santiago de Cuba.

1955
Castro is released from prison and exiled to Mexico.

1956
Castro and a band of rebel followers land in Oriente Province and go underground in the Sierra Maestra.

1957
Castro's forces win the first of many victories over Batista's army.

1959
Batista flees Cuba; Castro takes command of the government; the Agrarian Reform Law goes into effect.

1960
The Urban Reform Law goes into effect; upper- and middle-class Cubans begin emigrating; Cuba signs a major trade agreement with the Soviet Union; Cuba nationalizes American holdings on the island; the United States declares a trade embargo against Castro's Cuba; the Federation of Cuban Women is founded.

1961
CIA-trained Cuban exiles stage a failed invasion at the Bay of Pigs; Castro declares Cuba a Socialist state.

1962
Cuba is expelled from the Organization of American States (OAS); OAS members begin cutting trade relations with Cuba; food rationing in Cuba begins; the Cuban missile crisis brings the world to the brink of nuclear Armageddon.

1965
The Cuban Communist Party is officially founded; Che Guevara resigns from the Cuban government and goes to Bolivia to foment armed Socialist revolution.

1968
Cuban government nationalizes most private businesses.

1970
The Brigades of Militant Mothers for Education is founded to encourage women to enter the workforce.

1975
The OAS ends political and economic sanctions against Cuba; Castro sends Cuban troops to Angola to help the newly installed Socialist government repel an invasion by South Africa; the CIA admits having tried to assassinate Castro eight times.

1976
Cuba adopts a new, Socialist constitution; the Family Code, which seeks to strengthen families while encouraging women to work outside the home, goes into law.

1977
Castro sends Cuban troops to Ethiopia to help the Socialist government repel an invasion by Somalia.

1979
For the first time, Cuban émigrés are allowed to visit their relatives in Cuba.

1980
One hundred twenty-five thousand Cubans leave for the United States via the port of Mariel; free farmers' markets are opened.

1981
Cuban-American National Foundation (CANF) is founded by Cuban émigrés in the United States, from where it finances and supports counterrevolutionary activity in Cuba; U.S. president Ronald Reagan threatens to invade Cuba.

1985
A new housing law that allows renters to purchase their living quarters goes into effect; the Cuban government opens the Office for Religious Affairs as a means of improving church-state relations.

1986
Farmers' markets are closed down.

1987
The infant mortality rate drops to the lowest in Latin America, while life expectancy rises to the highest.

1989
European communism begins to collapse, thus bringing on the Special Period in Cuba; the Castro regime begins promoting tourism as a way to earn income.

1991
The Soviet Union splits apart, costing Cuba its best trading partner.

1993
Cuba legalizes the use of U.S. dollars as currency in Cuba; the Castro regime permits Cubans to open their own small businesses; state farms replace worker-managed cooperative farms.

1994
Farmers' markets reopen.

1997
Terrorists linked to the CANF attack several Cuban hotels and restaurants.

1998
Pope John Paul II visits Cuba.

2002
Former U.S. president Jimmy Carter visits Cuba.

For Further Research

Primary Sources

Paul D. Bethel, *The Losers: The Definitive Report, by an Eyewitness, of the Communist Conquest of Cuba and the Soviet Penetration in Latin America.* New Rochelle, NY: Arlington House, 1969.

Ernesto Cardenal, *In Cuba.* New York: New Directions, 1974.

Fidel Castro, *History Will Absolve Me.* New York: Lyle Stuart, 1961.

Andrei Codrescu, *Ay, Cuba! A Socio-Erotic Journey.* New York: St. Martin's, 1999.

Carlo Gebler, *Driving Through Cuba: An East-West Journey.* London: Abacus, 1988.

Orlando Castro Hidalgo, *Spy for Fidel.* Miami: E.A. Seemann, 1971.

Christopher Hunt, *Waiting for Fidel.* Boston: Houghton Mifflin, 1998.

Martin Kenner and James Petras, eds., *Fidel Castro Speaks.* New York: Grove, 1969.

George Lavan, ed., *Che Guevara Speaks: Selected Speeches and Writings.* New York: Pathfinder, 1967.

José Luis Llovio-Menéndez, *Insider: My Hidden Life as a Revolutionary in Cuba.* New York: Bantam, 1988.

Lee Lockwood, *Castro's Cuba, Cuba's Fidel: An American Journalist's Inside Look at Today's Cuba.* New York: Macmillan, 1967.

Julio García Luis, *Cuban Revolutionary Reader: A Documentary History of Forty Key Moments of the Cuban Revolution.* London: Ocean Press, 2001.

Neill Macauley, *A Rebel in Cuba: An American's Memoir.* Chicago: Quadrangle, 1970.

Judy Maloof, ed., *Voices of Resistance: Testimonies of Cuban and Chilean Women.* Lexington: University Press of Kentucky, 1999.

Frank Mankiewicz and Kirby Jones, *With Fidel: A Portrait of Castro and Cuba.* New York: Ballantine, 1975.

John Martino with Nathaniel Weyl, *I Was Castro's Prisoner: An American Tells His Story.* New York: Devin-Adair, 1963.

Tony Mendoza, *Cuba—Going Back.* Austin: University of Texas Press, 1997.

C. Peter Ripley, *Conversations with Cuba.* Athens: University of Georgia Press, 1999.

Andrew Salkey, *Havana Journal.* Baltimore: Penguin, 1971.

Pedro Pérez Sarduy and Jean Stubbs, eds., *Afro-Cuban Voices: On Race and Identity in Contemporary Cuba.* Gainesville: University Press of Florida, 2000.

Elizabeth Sutherland, *The Youngest Revolution: A Personal Report on Cuba.* New York: Dial, 1969.

Secondary Sources

Moises Asis, *Judaism in Cuba, 1959–1999.* Coral Gables, FL: Institute for Cuban and Cuban-American Studies, School of International Studies, University of Miami, 2000.

Sahadeo Basdeo and Heather N. Nicol, *Canada, the United States, and Cuba: An Evolving Relationship.* London: Eurospan, 2002.

James G. Blight and Philip Brenner, *Sad and Luminous Days: Cuba's Struggle with the Superpowers After the Missile Crisis.* Lanham, MD: Rowman & Littlefield, 2002.

Yvonne M. Conde, *Operation Pedro Pan: The Untold Exodus of 14,048 Cuban Children.* London: Routledge, 2000.

Laura J. Enriquez, *Cuba's New Agricultural Revolution: The Transformation of Food Crop Production in Contemporary Cuba.* Oakland, CA: Food First Institute for Food and Development Policy, 2000.

Clive Foss, *Fidel Castro*. Stroud, Gloucestershire, England: Sutton, 2000.

Irving L. Horowitz and Jaime Suchlicki, *Cuban Communism, 1959–2003*. New Brunswick, NJ: Transaction, 2003.

Antoni Kapcia, *Cuba: Island of Dreams*. New York: Berg, 2000.

Alexandra Keeble, *In the Spirit of Wandering Teachers: Cuba's Literacy Campaign, 1961*. London: Ocean, 2001.

Peter Kross, *Target Fidel: A Narrative Encyclopedia on the U.S. Government's Plot to Kill Fidel Castro, 1959–1965*. Franklin Park, NJ: Kross, 1999.

E. Wright Ledbetter, Ambrosio Fornet, and Louis A. Pérez Jr., *Cuba: Picturing Change*. Albuquerque: University of New Mexico Press, 2002.

Thomas M. Leonard, *Castro and the Cuban Revolution*. Westport, CT: Greenwood, 1999.

Manuel Piñeiro Losada and Luis Suárez Salazar, *Che Guevara and the Latin American Revolutionary Movements*. London: Ocean, 2001.

Catherine Murphy, *Cultivating Havana: Urban Agriculture and Food Security in the Years of Crisis*. Oakland, CA: Food First Institute for Food and Development Policy, 1999.

Marifeli Pérez-Stable, *The Cuban Revolution: Origins, Course, and Legacy*. New York: Oxford University Press, 1999.

Robert E. Quirk, *Fidel Castro: The Full Story of His Rise to Power, His Regime, His Allies, and His Adversaries*. New York: W.W. Norton, 1993.

Ramón Eduardo Ruiz, *Cuba: The Making of a Revolution*. Amherst: University of Massachusetts Press, 1968.

Julia E. Sweig, *Inside the Cuban Revolution: Fidel Castro and the Urban Underground*. Cambridge, MA: Harvard University Press, 2002.

Hugh S. Thomas, *Cuba: The Pursuit of Freedom.* London: Picador, 2001.

Hugh S. Thomas, Georges A. Fauriol, and Juan Carlos Weiss, *The Cuban Revolution Twenty-Five Years Later.* Boulder, CO: Westview, 1984.

Angelo Trento, *Castro and Cuba: From the Revolution to the Present.* New York: Interlink, 2000.

María López Vigil, *Cuba: Neither Heaven nor Hell.* Washington, DC: EPICA, 1999.

Index